The Legend of Aleister Crowley

Some Other Titles From New Falcon Publications

Aha! The Sevenfold Mystery of the Ineffable Love   **By Aleister Crowley**
Undoing Yourself with Energized Meditation and other Devices
Secrets of Western Tantra: The Sexuality of the Middle Path
Dogma Daze   **By Christopher S. Hyatt, Ph.D.**
Rebels & Devils; The Psychology of Liberation
       Edited by Christopher S. Hyatt, Ph.D.
Aleister Crowley's Illustrated Goetia
Taboo: Sex, Religion & Magick
Sex Magic, Tantra & Tarot: The Way of the Secret Lover
       By Christopher S. Hyatt, Ph.D., and Lon Milo DuQuette
Pacts With The Devil
Urban Voodoo: A Beginner's Guide to Afro-Caribbean Magic
       By Jason Black and Christopher S. Hyatt, Ph.D.
The Psychopath's Bible   **By Christopher S. Hyatt, Ph.D., and Dr. Jack Willis**
Ask Baba Lon   **By Lon Milo DuQuette**
Lucifer's Rebellion: A Tribute to Christopher S. Hyatt, Ph.D.
       Edited with a Foreword By Shelley Marmor
Aleister Crowley and the Treasure House of Images
  By J.F.C. Fuller, Aleister Crowley, Lon Milo DuQuette and Nancy Wasserman
Enochian World of Aleister Crowley **By Lon Milo DuQuette and Aleister Crowley**
Info-Psychology   *Neuropolitique*   *The Game of Life*
What Does WoMan Want?   **By Timothy Leary, Ph.D.**
Healing Energy, Prayer and Relaxation
The Complete Golden Dawn System of Magic
The Portable Complete Golden Dawn System of Magic
The Golden Dawn Audio CDs
What You Should Know About The Golden Dawn
The Eye in the Triangle: An Interpretation of Aleister Crowley
The Legend of Aleister Crowley   **By Dr. Israel Regardie**
Rebellion, Revolution and Religiouness   **By Osho**
Zen Without Zen Masters   **By Camden Benares**
Beyond Duality: The Art of Transcendence   **By Laurence Galian**
Reichian Therapy: A Practical Guide for Home Use   **By Dr. Jack Willis**
Woman's Orgasm: A Guide to Sexual Satisfaction
       By Benjamin Graber M.D. and Georgia Kline-Graber R.N.
The Dream Illuminati   *The Illuminati of Immortality*   **By Wayne Saalman**
An Insider's Guide to Robert Anton Wilson   **By Eric Wagner**
Shaping Formless Fire   *Seizing Power*   *Taking Power*   **By Stephen Mace**
Lovecraft Lexicon   **By Anthony Pearsall**
The Everyday Atheist   **By Ronald F. Murphy**
The Illuminati Conspiracy: The Sapiens System   **By Donald Holmes, M.D.**

Many of our titles are now available on Kindle!!!

Please visit our website at http://www.newfalcon.com

The Legend of Aleister Crowley

By Israel Regardie
and P.R. Stephensen

NEW FALCON PUBLICATIONS
LAS VEGAS, NEVADA, U.S.A.

This single edition of 500 copies is published
under license by the copyright owners,
Ordo Templi Orientis Incorporated (Australia)
and limited to 500 copies.
For sale only in the USA.

All rights reserved. No part of this book, in part or in whole, may be reproduced, transmitted, or utilized, in any form or by any means, electronic or mechanical, including photocopying, recording, or by any information storage and retrieval system, without permission in writing from the publisher, except for brief quotations in critical articles, books and reviews.

International Standard Book Number: 1-56184-550-7

First Edition 1930
Second Edition 1970
Third Edition 1983
Fourth Revised Edition 2015

The paper used in this publication meets the minimum requirements of the American National Standard for Permanence of Paper for Printed Library Materials Z39.48-1984

NEW FALCON PUBLICATIONS
9550 South Eastern Avenue • Suite 253
Las Vegas, NV 89123
www.newfalcon.com
email: info@newfalcon.com

I gladly dedicate
this Legend to my good friend
GRADY L. McMURTRY
Caliph of the O.T.O.

Contents

Foreward by Lon Milo DuQuette, 2015	*i*
Introduction by Israel Regardie, 1969	*xi*
CHAPTER I The Man Crowley	1
CHAPTER II Early Period, 1896-1907	25
CHAPTER III "Equinox" Period, 1908-1914	65
CHAPTER IV The War	111
CHAPTER V After the War	143
Epilogue	183

Foreword

Look! It doesn't matter if Crowley was a Satanist, he was a good kind of Satanist, and you'll just love him! Trust me.
—*Robert (Mad Bob) Patton*

You've probably heard *things* about Aleister Crowley (1875–1947). Perhaps you've heard monstrous things–hideous things–terrifying things–disgusting and ghastly things. On the other hand, you might have heard wonderful things–funny things–astonishing things–inspiring things–even supernatural and sacred things? Anyone who thinks they know something about Crowley will most likely voice a very strong opinion either unfavorable or favorable.

Detractors are quick to vilify him as the Devil himself–insane, perverse, and evil; while his admirers lionize him as a genius; an enlightened holy man; a saint; a Buddha; *Prophet of a New Aeon*. It's been nearly seventy years since Edward Alexander (Aleister) Crowley drew his last breath, and opinions about him remain as passionately polarized as they were in 1930 when *The Legend of Aleister Crowley* was first published.

As you will learn in Dr. Regardie's fine introductory words (penned in 1969), this slim little volume was originally written and compiled by Crowley's friend and publisher, P.R. Stephensen, to serve as a testament *to* (and showcase sampler *of*) Crowley's extraordinary talents and contributions to the world of English literature and philosophy. The book was also an undisguised attempt to mount a rational defense of Crowley's character and reputation that had been mercilessly and irrationally attacked by the press since the turn of the century. Stephensen's efforts to redeem Crowley, however, would not be immediately or universally successful. It saddens me to say that today, eighty-five years after its initial publication, the world needs to read this book more than ever.

The Legend of Aleister Crowley was my first *real* introduction to the personality and works of Aleister Crowley. I first read it at a pivotal season in my own life, shortly after our son was born in 1972. To say it was a watershed moment in my life would be a monumental understatement. I would go on to spend the better part of the next forty years of my life studying Crowley; digesting his writings; meeting and learning from people who had known him when he was alive; practicing his magical and meditation techniques, and attempting to live the philosophy of life he so passionately espoused. However, my first few stumbling encounters with the works of the man who called himself the *Beast 666* were awkward and comically terrifying.

I was a 24-year old failed yogi and fledgling western mystic poseur working my way through the monographs of the *Rosicrucian Order, AMORC*[1], the *Traditional Martinist Order*[2], and

---

[1] The Ancient and Mystical Order Rose Crucis (AMORC), headquartered at the time in San Jose, California. Established in 1915 by Harvey Spenser Lewis who claimed the organization was the modern incarnation of the ancient Rose-Croix Order (Rosicrucians) which, in turn, was the continuation of the mystery schools of ancient Egypt.

[2] The Traditional Martinist Order (TMO), a mystical order of Christian Mystics who follow one branch of the teachings of French philosopher, Louis-Claude de Saint-Martin. At the time of my involvement TMO was closely aligned with the Rosicrucian Order (AMORC).

the *Builders of the Adytum*[3]. I fancied myself a bit of a heretic and spiritual rebel, but I certainly wanted nothing to do with anything that smacked of black magick or Satanism[4].

Everything I had read about Aleister Crowley up to that point was bad. My occult dictionary listed him as a black magician who ate human flesh and sacrificed 120 babies one year. My blue-haired Rosicrucian elders told me he was the devil himself. My fellow Martinists cautioned me not to even utter his name. My tarot-loving friends in the BOTA warned me that his teachings were sexually perverse, and that he advocated performing grotesque and unnatural sexual acts on tarot cards. But, for some curious reason, the more my mystical colleagues tried to dissuade me, the more fascinated I became. Who was this guy?

As I have written elsewhere, I bought a deck of his *Thoth Tarot* cards...then, hysterically gave them away...then, took them back after talking with Mad Bob, our family friend (and spiritual mentor) who soundly upbraided me for my display spiritual cowardice.

"Crowley was cool. He was a genius and a holy man. If you're really serious about mastering magick and the Hermetic arts you're going to have to dig deep into what this guy's about."

---

[3] The Builders of the Adytum (B.O.T.A.) is primarily a correspondence school of the Western mystery tradition which traces its roots and traditions to the Hermetic Order of the Golden Dawn and esoteric Freemasonry. Founded by Paul Foster Case in 1922 and based in Los Angeles, California, it was led at the time of my involvement by Case's successor, Ann Davies. B.O.T.A. focuses primarily on the Hermetic Qabalah and the qabalistic aspecst of the Tarot.

[4] At the time I was an ignorant and superstitious young fool who had no idea that "Black Magick" and "Satanism" (as I fearfully imagined them to be) did not exist in objective reality. Today, while I do not call myself either a black magician or Satanist or even care to use the terms to describe what I believe or practice, I know quite a few perfectly brilliant and intelligent individuals who are quite comfortable identifying themselves as such. Everyone I've met are honest and sincere, and in my opinion, as liberated and possessed of high moral integrity as those who follow less colorful and exotic spiritual paths.

"But everyone says he was a Satanist. Was he a Satanist?" I asked Bob.

"*No*. He wasn't a Satanist!" Then he paused. "Well, *Yes*. I guess you could say he was." Then he disagreed with himself once more. "No…not really!" Finally he said, *"Look! It doesn't matter if Crowley was a Satanist, he was a good kind of Satanist, and you'll just love him! Trust me."*

I took Bob at his word, and soon after our curious conversation I had the opportunity to read Crowley's *The Book of Thoth*, the work that was written late in his life to accompany the *Thoth Tarot* cards. I felt like a grammar-school student trying to read post-graduate papers on magick, philosophy, alchemy, qabalah, astrology, and comparative religion. Even though I understood only a fraction of a fraction of what I read I found Crowley to be brilliant, funny, and someone who had obviously mastered the spiritual arts of which he wrote so passionately. Furthermore it became breathtakingly evident to that Crowley had actually achieved the expanded levels of consciousness his magical practices and meditations are designed to trigger.

Crowley was the real deal, I thought. And if that means he was a Satanist, then he was a good kind of Satanist…and I just loved him!

The Book of Thoth, and the *Thoth Tarot* cards however, provided precious little information about who Crowley was; what his background was; why he was so admired and hated. I wanted to know more. At the time, books by and about Crowley were very rare if they existed at all. One afternoon in a Laguna Beach bookstore a beautiful black cat named Catalina guided me to an odd little book that would provide me a clearer picture of Crowley the man, the poet, and the philosopher.

"Any books by Aleister Crowley?"[5] I asked the owner.

She looked at me as if I asked her for a book about baby torture, and answered that she didn't think she had any Crowley but pointed to the cat sleeping serenely on the second shelf of the bookcase in the adjacent room. "If I have anything it will be in the shelf behind Catalina...that is, if you can get her to move."

Sure enough, peeking just behind the somewhat obese feline was what appeared to be a damaged paperbound edition of *The Legend of Aleister Crowley*. It didn't look at all impressive or scary. In fact it looked rather shoddily produced–the cover almost bare of adornment or color with only a simple graphic of *eye in a triangle* and the words:

THE LEGEND OF
ALEISTER CROWLY[6]

By
P.R. Stephensen
and
Israel Regardie

PROPHET OF A NEW AEON
vilified as
THE MOST EVIL MAN IN THE WORLD

Who and what is Aleister Crowley that he should be the original of a legend of infamy without parallel in the modern world?

Here is the evidence of a campaign of personal vilification unparalleled in literary history.

Here too, is Crowley himself–
through his own words, his books, his life.

---

[5] At the time I was still incorrectly pronouncing Crowley's name "Craw-lee" instead of "Crow-ley" (which rhymes with Holy).

[6] This particular edition was a 1970 Llewellyn Publications paperback reprint of the 1930 Mandrake Press first edition. In 1930 P.R. Stephensen was the publisher of Mandrake Press.

"Prophet of a New Aeon"?
"The Most Evil Man in the World"?
"Infamy"?
Cool!

I have to confess the titillating language of the crudely-printed blurbs on the cover intrigued me no end. I stroked Catalina and thanked her, then immediately purchased the book from the shocked proprietor and rushed home to read it.

I was especially impressed with the *Introduction* by Israel Regardie (1907 – 1985). I recognized the name because I had already read his classic text, *The Tree of Life*[7] as part of my self-guided efforts to learn the qabalah. He had been Crowley's secretary in the late 1920s and lived and with him in France and Germany during an especially colorful period in Crowley's life.

Regardie was just a couple years older than my own father and so in my eyes represented a generational link between Crowley and me. His frank, contemporary writing style was pleasantly palatable and served to lift the verbose, intimidating, larger-than-life Crowley out of the fog of superstitious mythology and place him in the clear objective light of psychology and philosophy. Knowing that this respected and august author thought so highly of Crowley was very reassuring, and the fact he put his seal of approval on this little book profoundly elevated its importance in my estimation.

The signature line of Regardie's *Introduction* revealed that he lived in Studio City, California a little over 50 miles

---

[7] Israel Regardie, *The Tree of Life: a Study in Magick*. NY: Samuel Weiser). 1972 reprint of the 1932 first edition.

from Costa Mesa where I lived. Suddenly the vaporous fancies of magical history and legend crystallized into the objective space-time coordinates of my own backyard. "Perhaps I could actually meet this guy someday." I thought. (Indeed, the gods soon conspired to make this fantasy a reality. In less than two years I found myself sitting in Regardie's living room in Study City sipping champagne cocktails and discussing magick and Aleister Crowley with my magical neighbor-hero. Regardie and I remained friends until his death in 1985.)

I don't have to remind the reader that 1972 was a long time ago, and the world has changed dramatically in the last thirty-five years. Crowley's reputation, if not totally redeemed, has undergone a fairer, more balanced evaluation in the court of public opinion (at least among the educated and well-informed). Books *by* Crowley and *about* Crowley are abundant and readily available around the world and in many languages. His teachings and occult organizations flourish worldwide, and his contributions to modern art, literature, and philosophy are increasingly acknowledged and recognized.

In 2002 the BBC aired a television documentary, "Great Britons", based on a poll the network conducted to learn who the British people considered the top one hundred "greatest British people in history." There, in 73rd place (nestled comfortably between King Henry V (of Shakespeare fame) and Robert the Bruce (of Mel Gibson's Braveheart fame), was occultist, ceremonial magician, poet, painter, novelist and mountaineer–ALEISTER CROWLEY.

I will close by heartily encouraging the reader to make the effort if he or she wishes to learn more about Crowley. For me, my labor these last forty years has been well repaid, and my life, my consciousness, and (I dare say…my spiritual happiness) has been enriched by the life, the teachings, the magick, and the extraordinary *legend* of Aleister Crowley. I encourage anyone wishing a more thorough and scholarly comment on *The Legend of Aleister Crowley*…to also obtain and read Mr. Stephen King's excellent 2007 edition published by Helios Books; and to also avail themselves of Israel Regardie's own biography of Crowley, *The Eye in the Triangle*, published by New Falcon Publications.

Lon Milo DuQuette

July 4, 2015
Costa Mesa, California

Introduction

It was in the Spring of the year 1929 that the Surete Generale sprung a surprise on the unsuspecting Crowley menage. Aleister Crowley had been living in Paris with his mistress, Marie de Miramar. I had moved from a small hotel nearby into the apartment on Avenue de Suffren in the *XVI* arrondissement, serving as his secretary. We were all handed expulsion papers. Leave with twenty-four hours!

Crowley immediately pleaded illness to gain time to institute legal proceedings of some kind to reverse the expulsion. De Miramar and I had no recourse but to follow the terms of the *Refus de Sejour* and we wound up in Brussels to await the arrival of Crowley.

Finally realizing that there was no shaking the intransigeant attitude of the Surete Generale, he cast off the dust of Paris from his shoes. In Brussels he was persuaded to join some of his fervent disciples in Berlin. The problem was how to get both de Miramar and myself there.

Having been expelled from France and refused admittance to England (as narrated at some length in *The Eye in the Triangle*), we all had serious doubts about the German authorities permitting us entry. So Crowley decided to marry de Miramar, thinking that would facilitate her entry into Germany.

But that wasn't easy in Brussels; so much red tape surrounded a marriage of foreigners on Belgian soil. But since the subject of marriage had been raised, it persisted despite the difficulties raised by the Belgians. He took a chance on taking de Miramar with him to Berlin to get married there. The chance paid off. I was to stay on in Brussels typing an additional set of copies of *The Confessions* for ultimate publication. This was forty years ago!

After a successful summer in Berlin, Crowley and his wife returned to England. This time there was no problem about her admission, since she had married a Briton. While in London, he met the proprietors of the Mandrake Press on Museum Street. One of them, P. R. Stephensen, had previous experience in the book business, having run the Fanfrolico Press a bit earlier with a writer named James Lindsay I believe, producing some handsomely printed, bound and illustrated books. He became so enthusiastic over much of Crowley's writing that he persuaded his partner, named Goldston or Goldstein, I cannot remember which, to start a publishing program of Crowley's works. In quick succession, *The Stratagem, Moonchild,* and the first two volumes of a projected six volume set of *The Confessions of Aleister Crowley* came off the press.

While this publishing program was under way, Crowley, who was far from a well man, moved out of London to a little town in Ken named Knockholt. Stephensen had rented a house there. I imagine it was Stephensen who persuaded Crowley to rent a house there also. This was to facilitate possible discussion relative to the Crowley publication program.

I managed to gain entry into England towards the end of the year 1929, perhaps in November, and immediately joined Crowley in Knockholt, about thirty miles or so south of

London. There I found Crowley ill with a severe bout of phlebitis, while Marie suffered with colitis, boredom and loneliness, and excessive drinking.

We all suffered from boredom in Knockholt. To relieve this, Crowley and I played chess a good deal. I managed to have time to read every book and manuscript I could lay hands on that Crowley had written. In this manner, I have acquired an almost encyclopedic view of Crowley's literary output. Marie coped with her boredom not only through the ingestion of alcohol, but by painting with oils, a pretty messy and unproductive business.

It was not a serene household by any means. Every now and again, I succeeded in getting out of the house, walking down the street to where the Stephensen's lived. I never knew what P. R. stood for, but Winifred, his wife, called him Inky— and Inky he was to all of us. They were very charming and kind people, and I have spent many a pleasant hour and even afternoon there, playing chess with Inky, talking a great deal, and receiving the benefit of their generous Australian hospitality.

Inky's interest in Aleister Crowley was wholly literary. He had had a good grounding in philosophy, but cared absolutely nothing for the occult. He was amusedly tolerant of my interest in magick and yoga and inner growth and development, but it was without serious meaning to him. He was a good-natured, kind, generous human being who enjoyed living, mental stimulation, good food and drink, sex, and fine literature, especially if the latter had been produced in beautiful editions.

Meantime, it seems as though the Mandrake Press was running into a great deal of stiff opposition from the booksellers both in London and England as a whole. They wanted nothing to do with Crowley. His reputation had been thoroughly blackened by the exposé conducted by James Douglas in the *Sunday Express* years earlier when Collins had first published Crowley's *Diary of a Drug Fiend*. His expulsion from Italy did his reputation no good, nor was the recent expulsion from France any great help. Sales were poor, and Goldstein was getting worried. After all, he had put up the capital, and there was not much of a return.

This put Stephensen in a very awkward position. He was still enthused about the excellent quality of Crowley's writing, and wanted to continue publishing. He and Crowley discussed this at some length. Since, in Crowley's home, there was the big scrap-book of press reviews and notices, it struck Inky that Mandrake's selling position might be enhanced if he compiled a book using these book-reviews as a defense of Crowley against current sales resistance.

Inky was a good writer. He had done a great deal of ghost-writing both before and after this particular book *The Legend*. In fact, a couple of years afterwards, when Crowley had wandered off to Germany again, I helped Inky in his ghosting of two other books—one on the life of Anna Pavlova by her former musical director, and another on fox-hounds and fox-hunting by a master of hounds in South Kent. This was fun. I learned a lot from him for which I am most indebted. I hope, wherever he is, he may read this so that he can learn of my appreciation and gratitude to him.

Crowley, as it were, loaned me to Stephensen to help him with the proposed book. Inky had the skill of the writer. Crowley had the scrap-book. I had the broad familiarity with Crowely's writing. So Inky went to work dictating to me with my Stenotype. We worked daily and steadfastly.

I cannot recall now how long it actually took to write this book, but it was not very long. Months previously I had been asked to make a précis of Crowley's lengthy article "The Last Straw" originally published in *The International* when he was the editor during the War years. It was included in the text of *The Legend*. When completed it served as a splendid recapitulation of Crowley's literary reception by the British and world press. Inky used the scrapbook to superb advantage, working into it both favorable and adverse criticisms so that a colorful tapestry was woven, proving to the British booksellers how utterly mistaken they were in showing antagonism to this new Crowley release. It turned out to be a good book. Even today, forty years after the event, it still reads well and so deserves to be re-issued.

However, in 1930, when it first came out, it reluctantly sold out a small first edition—and that was the end. It never really got off the ground. Nor did it eradicate the booksellers' refusal to handle Crowley. The Mandrake Press went down the drain.

Goldstein got fed up and pulled out from the Mandrake Press; the partnership was dissolved. It was invested in by some Crowley disciples who then took in a couple of ex-Army men who professed to be financiers. Under their able jurisdiction, the poor Mandrake Press was first incorporated and, shortly afterwards, liquidated.

Inky withdrew to Knockholt, did some more ghosting, and ultimately returned to Australia, his native land. Many years afterwards, I received a letter from him relative to Crowley, still demonstrating his high regard for the latter's literary work. Inky never fell out with Crowley as had so many of the latter's friends and associates. The contact had been too short really.

Inky was able to retain his high regard and respect for the "old man" as we familiarly called him.

This is 1969. The world has changed a great deal since then. The hippies have come—but not quite gone. In the meantime, they have left an indelible impress on our culture. Part of this impress bears all the earmarks of a Crowley revival. The result is a vast interest in Crowley's books which now command a high premium, money wise, when they are at all possible to obtain—which is not very often. Most of those who own Crowley literature usually hang on to it, but little of it finding its way to used bookstores.

Crowley died in 1947. Why he appointed John Symonds as one of his literary executors is a mystery that never will be divined. It is perhaps another example of Crowley's poor judgment about people. Symonds wrote a disgusting book over a decade ago entitled *The Great Beast*. It is a malicious, contemptible piece of work crammed with deliberate misinterpretation and ignorant misunderstanding of what Crowley stood for. This wretched work was followed by another, *The Magick of Aleister Crowley*. In this second book, Symonds has extrapolated from the diaries and other works by Crowley in such a contemptible manner as to make "the old man" look like a complete idiot.

Not content with this insolence, Symonds has steadfastly refused permission to me and several other writers to use any of Crowley's published material. Evidently he has assumed that his literary executorship, instituted on behalf of and for the benefit of the Ordo Templi Orientis, should be used for his own personal gain. Recently he has written an introduction to *The Confessions* just published in England by Jonathan Cape Ltd., and which will be published early in 1970 in the United States by Hill & Wang Inc. This introduction shows a modification of his earlier stand on Crowley. While not at all complimentary, it is not so devastatingly critical of Crowley. I have to admit that his editing of *The Confessions* is not bad. For this he needs some little applause—but not too much.

I have suggested to Llewellyn Publications that this *Legend of Aleister Crowley* be republished because the English reviews of *The Confessions* show that the old intransigeant attitude towards Crowley has not altered throughout the years. He is still regarded as the "bad boy of English journalism."

Curiously enough, I have just received a letter from a psychiatrist friend in England who recently read *The Confessions*, about which he could only remark:

> I am struck by Crowley's brilliance, the vividness of his thought, his picturesque language, his great sense of humour, the energy that he put into life—in fact, there is more than a bit of manic restlessness in his make-up. But what is the difference anyway—between mild and well-controlled manic energy and healthy enthusiasm?

This professional point of view is worth remembering as I follow Inky's original example to quote from some contemporary reviewers of *The Confessions of Aleister Crowley*.

The Times Literary Supplement dated 23 October 1969, had a very long review of the book, which would have pleased Crowley no end. It appeared on the first page, running over onto the second. The review, without a byline, says:

> The reader may thus approach Crowley himself either as Ipsissimus, the incarnation of the Logos of the New Aeon, or as a human enigma.

It then proceeds quite fairly to enumerate some of the egotistical extravagances of Crowley in these words:

> He was dazzled by his multi-faceted brilliance. With Oscar Eckenstein, he shared the glory of being superior to all other mountaineers. He was a master of chess (half-blue at Cambridge). He was the equal of Shakespeare as a poet, a novelist and shorty-story writer of sublimity, a traveller in the physical and spiritual worlds as adventurous as Sir Richard Burton, a psychologist more profound than his coeval Freud, a scientific magician in the tradition of the greatest masters but humbly their superior because he had been chosen by the gods through his Holy Guardian Angel to initiate the new Aeon of God the Child. He was an aristocrat, knighted by Don Carlos, etc., etc.,

The rest of the review is taken up with exposing some of his less admirable character traits, terminating with:

> The authorities, and the general public, viewed Crowley with justifiable mistrust. He was as much the epitome of all disharmony and confusion as the demon Chronozon of his evocation. He was mad, bad, and dangerous to know. But this was not because he was deliberately evil. It was something far more sinister and dangerous. The Logos of the New Aeon, he sincerely believed that, having crossed the Abyss, he was beyond good and evil; and frankly he didn't give a damn for the whole human race. They were nothing but a pack of cards.
>
> What a Joker he was!

In the whole two page review, there is not one single line to be construed as favorable to Crowley's work or reputation. It is a lengthy denunciation, veiled certainly, but just as destructive in its own way as were the original full page editorial ravings of James Douglas in *The Sunday Express*.

The Listener of the same date is hardly more complimentary. The reviewer, whose name is D. J. Enright, begins with an anecdote about a second-hand bookstore where he had picked up a book by Conrad which bore Crowley's autograph on the flyleaf. It had been marked down several times, leading him to comment:

> The declining market-value of Crowley's autograph indicates the low esteem into which he had fallen before his death in 1947. This 'autohagiography' is unlikely to establish him as anything more than another English Eccentric, *fin-de-siecle* variety, graded unsuitable for promotion by the British Council.

Maybe! So far as the declining market-value of Crowley's books are concerned, let me put on record the fact that many years ago a set of the *Equinox* might be obtained for $100 for the ten volumes. Since all my Crowley books were burgled from my home at the end of February 1969, a local bookseller offered me a week ago the first volume of the *Equinox* for $45,000!

Enright does try to fair. For example, he wrote:

> Crowley is by no means a figure of fun, and much of this book (though far from all its 1,000 pages) is extremely readable. Besides being many other and different things, he was a bit of a John Bull, a man of common sense and forthright response, with a

British contempt for British hypocrisy. He was a tireless and fearless traveller, especially in the East, refusing to avail himself of the advice and assistance customarily proferred by HM Consuls, and like many other Britons he considered the Mohammedans vastly superior to all other brands of native life. Like many other Britons too, he only began to warm to the Chinese when a mandarin invited him to a banquet at which "the opulence of Trimalchio was concealed beneath the refinement of Lucullus and the culture of Horace." Rather less Britishly, he admired the coolies because their performance proved the harmlessness of opium. "I timed the men under the worst conditions and they did eight miles without rest in two hours dead. If those men were 'physical wreaks from the abuse of opium' I should like to see the animal in his undamaged state!"

Regarding Crowley's mountain-climbing exploits in Switzerland, Mexico and India, the reviewer was forced to add:

> It seems that he really was a serious and an intrepid climber. The general reader, with a salt-sprinkler to hand, will find this part of his story, along with his travels, the most palatable—and the chapters on Magick the least palatable, if only because human kind cannot bear very much unreality.

On the whole, Enright is pretty just, commenting fairly accurately on direct quotations from Crowley's book with regard to Liber Legis, his relations with women, and his patronizing attitude towards his disciples and followers.

But the sheer arrogance which makes Crowley's confessions initially so readable begins to pall.

A revealing story concerns Victor Neuburg, one of his most faithful followers, who later achieved a rather less ambiguous fame as the discoverer of Dylan Thomas, whose early poems he printed in *The Sunday Referee*...

As the book goes on, and Crowley becomes increasingly involved in the occult, so it grows increasingly repellent...While Crowley continues with little self-pity to represent himself as a genius misunderstood, he displays his closest associates as unequivocally squalid or foolish, as weaklings, drunkards, drug-addicts, swindlers, pimps, perverts.... Perhaps the world is fortunate in that he felt nothing but contempt for secular politics.

There was another review entitled "Emperor of Hocus-Pocus" under the byline of Maurice Richardson which appeared in *The Observer Review* on the 26 October 1969. This is wholly unfavorable and critical all the way through. Its tenor can best be appreciated by a single remark in the first column:

Sensation-seekers will get better value as well as a clearer, more rounded account in John Symond's biography "The Great Beast".

About the middle of the review there is another paragraph which is indicative further of the general contemptuous attitude which this reviewer shares with John Symonds:

It is always difficult with megalomaniacal cranks to sort out fantasy and trickery from genuine delusion. It is particularly difficult in Crowley's case because he was not only manic and paranoid and often drugged to the eyes, but also an accomplished con-man....

The concluding sentence of the review is:

His great gas-bag of an ego which, like a true mystic, he thought he had annihilated, must have been a fearful inconvenience.

The Evening News of October 23, 1969 published a three column review headed in large black type by "A Beastly hard road to fame...." This appeared above a picture of Crowley taken from Equinox III, under which were two lines: "But Crowley would be glad he's not forgotten."

It too felt that John Symonds' cynical biography was far more informative and accurate than *The Confessions*. The tenor of the rest of the review can be deduced from that one piece of information.

The reviewer opened his dissertation with several lines in large type:

Glowering from between Mae West and an Indian guru in that spoof group photograph on the Sgt. Pepper's Lonely Hearts Club Band L.P. is a face with lard-like jowls and hot staring eyes. He looks furious at being there—the Great Beast cut down to Beatle size.

Later, he states:

He was a flamboyant showman and probably a black-mailer. He was a con-man on a splendid scale.... What is quickly apparent from the bombastic rigmarole is that the Beast was dotty.

It's concluding remark is:

Doubtless the Beast will be remembered for a long time, so I suppose his ambition came true. But it seems a beastly hard way to have achieved it.

So much for *The Evening News*.

The People, on the same date, published a review with enormous black capital letters under the byline of Tom Driberg. "The most Evil Man on Earth!" But this merely is a quotation from an earlier issue of *John Bull*, as Stephensen has shown in the text of *The Legend*.

Driberg is far from being altogether antagonistic, and seems capable of objective criticism and examination of matters in which he is not especially interested. For example:

> His basic commandment was "Do what thou wilt." Since his training in serious, formal magick (as he spelt it) was rigorous, he did not mean by this "Follow each casual impulse." He meant "Discover your own true will and do it." In other words, "Know yourself and be yourself."
>
> But such teaching is easily misunderstood and used as an excuse by the vicious or weak-minded—and Crowley...always had a few of them around.
>
> I first met Crowley when I was very young. He had asked me to lunch in London. I was curious, but distinctly on my guard.... The man I met was elderly, bald, stout, and dressed in good green Harris tweeds,— not at all exotic, except that, as we sat down, he said "Pardon me while I invoke the moon."
>
> Indeed, whenever I met him, he seemed normal and worldly—often worried about money, smoking Havana cigars or a pipe, a witty and congenial companion. It was hard to believe all the horrifying stories about him.... Crowley's funeral in 1947, at a municipal crematorium in Sussex, was as unusual as his life had been. Egyptian gods were invoked; Crowley's Hymn to Pan was recited.

The local councillors were deeply disturbed, and resolved that such a thing must not happen again.

I don't suppose it will.

Pat Williams in *The Sunday Telegraph* of October 26, 1969 has perhaps the most interesting, objective, and in many ways the most fair review of the lot. The opening paragraph is actually the theme of this introduction to *The Legend*, that the past dies very hard. People do not relinquish their impressions or memories of past events very readily.

The name of Aleister Crowley—the self-styled 'Beast 666'—still seems to evoke Satanic images 50-odd years after the heavy-breathing Press revelations of orgies and black masses in respectable metropolitan London.

Those images and revelations are going to haunt the public for a very long time, as well as to distort the reputation that Crowley really deserves.

The reviewer is lucid and insightful. Regarding the Law of Thelema, he asks:

> But what is will and whose is the law? The answer, on the evidence here, reveals a far higher intention than one might have expected. Crowley sought to align himself with hidden truths; the phrase was aimed, he says, at getting people to realise their essential selves, where they and the Godhead are one....

Which is not a bad commentary at all!

In Crowley, the braggart smothers the worshipper, the performer masks the priest, the wise man is not so much child as *enfant terrible*. Suicide and insanity were part of the wake he left in his magical and sexual (which were often identical) endeavours.

Yet one emerges even with a respect for his aspiration, his capacity, his hard work and his dedication, and there are things one can take from him.

Just prior to this respectful admission, there is an honest confession which says much for the reviewer. One could wish that many of the other reviewers had been able to accept this as simply as did Pat Williams.

> After nearly 1,000 pages I still don't know what to think of him.

And towards the end of the two column review, there is this final statement:

> ...a tale written with such conceit, flamboyance, panache, and energetic self-delight that it takes one's breath away.... That still leaves 500 further pages of contemporary gossip, mountaineering and travelling adventures...making it an appalling, fascinating read if you can stomach such swashbuckling swankiness.

Finally, on a note of almost despair, let me call attention to a notice which appeared in *The Psychic News* of November 1, 1969, written by Maurice Barbanell, one of the British stalwarts of the Spiritualist Movement. The notice, which is not a review, is headed 'Clown of the Occult'. I need only to quote a couple of very short paragraphs to give the reader the full flavor of Barbanell's liberal and enlightened attitudes:

> H. D. Ziman, whose review (in *The Daily Telegraph*) was headed 'Clown of the occult' said that

one of the troubles with this megalomaniac was that people were uncertain whether he meant to be taken seriously...

The new book describes how he varied lechery with taking immense does of drugs. I am sure that I don't want to read it.

It will be interesting to observe what will happen when Hill and Wang Inc., bring out the American edition of *The Confessions* early in 1970. At no time in his long career did Crowley ever succeed in making anything but the most superficial impression on English letters or the occult public. When he was domiciled in the U.S. during World War I, unfortunately it seems that the American literary scene and the American occult-reading public were even less affected by him than was England. It galled him no end. He became much more bitter and vitriolic about the U.S. than ever he had been about his native land, although admittedly a vast amount of his early poetry did condemn the narrowness and bigotry of the British people.

A great deal of what Crowley had to say in *The Confessions* about the United States is so evidently prejudicial, critical and destructive that it can easily be predicted that most of the American reviewers will have a field day. Probably they will seize upon some of these opinions to construct a monstrous reduplication of the aberrant English attitudes of fifty years ago. The current English reviews, as extrapolated above, will be as nothing to what we are likely to read when the American journalists get hold of *The Confessions*. I am far from happy about this prospect.

Admittedly Crowley was a show-off, an egotist, and an *enfant terrible*, as all the reviewers have indicated. But, with only an exception or two, they decline to perceive another aspect of the man which was a great mystic, sincere dedicated and hard working. He made demands on his students that in reality were not nearly as tough as those he made on himself—as the biography has shown. The reviewers became repelled by his self-adulation. Unfortunately, this prevented them from realizing that he really was a great poet, not necessarily the greatest as he claimed, nor on the same level as Shakespeare, but certainly a poet who has penned some immortal lines.

There is indeed ground for criticism of him. However, there is also ground for high praise of some of the things he has done. It is about time that the scale was struck and a balance achieved. For all too long—due in part to his own stupidity as perceived by Pat Williams in the lines "the braggart smothers the worshipper, the performer masks the priest, the wise man is not so much child as *enfant terrible*"— he has been wholly ignored and cruelly vilified. One has to agree with Stephensen that this history of vilification is without equal in literary history.

Despite everything, I am confident that the issuance of *The Confessions*, this *Legend of Aleister Crowley* and my own attempt at biography *The Eye in the Triangle* will accomplish some degree of restitution. They may do a little to right the wrong that has been done to a man of letters, a significantly religious though unorthodox man, a strong and valiant man, and restore him to the high place in history that he deserves.

Israel Regardie

December 15, 1969
Studio City, California

THE MAN CROWLEY

CHAPTER I

The Man Crowley

Aleister Crowley is a man. Many people would add, "What a man!" in tones either of extreme approval or, more usually, of extreme disapproval. I am anxious to avoid these extremes. I cannot properly dispute with people who say he is more than a man—one of the hierarchy of Those. Neither can I dispute on their own grounds with people who say he is something less than a man—a demon (to put it mildly) in human guise. Being no occultist, I am not able to settle such magical disputations. One of the strongest points in Crowley's favour is that he is undoubtedly a man.

Moreover, he is an interesting man, an extraordinary man; and, further, he is a dangerously good poet both in his poetry and in his life. Nothing much is known publicly about either of these activities. There is a great deal of dirty rumour. I am satisfied, after investigation, that rumour has lied, as usual; but more disgracefully and filthily than usual about this man.

For thirty years a certain spattering of mud has been thrown at him, and in recent years a complete barrage descended. Throwing mud at Aleister Crowley is quite a recognised branch of sport. What makes it easier is that he makes no attempt to dodge the muck. He seems to think it cannot reach him, that this muck, and these throwers of muck, are transient phenomena, unreal stuff, of no ascertainable cosmic significance. If a journalist writes three columns of abuse identifying him with Jack the Ripper, Crowley seems to take the attitude that nobody of intelligence will believe such arrant nonsense—and the others do not matter. It is possible that Crowley underestimates the amount of unintelligence in the world. He is a literary man of outstanding ability, yet he has never properly defended himself against scurrilous attacks from journalists like James Douglas and Horatio Bottomley. Is this because he believes they are not worth serious notice?

If so, he is loftily ignoring the fact that a great deal, a very great deal, of guttermud thrown, has stuck. Members of the "general public" who otherwise appear quite intelligent are definitely uneasy when Aleister Crowley is mentioned; think "there must be something in it all"; prefer to reply upon black rumour and blackguardly journalism for information about him; prefer to be "on the safe side" and to have nothing to do with Aleister Crowley. It is difficult to draw such people out in discussion. They don't wish to discuss the subject. Nevertheless they are prejudiced, definitely prejudiced, against Aleister Crowley. He is anathema and tabu.

Why? Who and what is Aleister Crowley that he should be the original of a legend of infamy without parallel in the modern world? That is the question which this little study sets out to investigate. Crowley is a strong poet, and strong poets are often unpopular. That morbid and quixotic inkslinger James Douglas referred only recently, with horror, to the "obese" Byron.

Probably Byron could have given James Douglas a least a half-way start in a swimming race across the Hellespont—club foot, alleged obesity, and all: most probably he could even have allowed James Douglas the use of a dinghy! And the same ink-slinging athlete has described Aleister Crowley as degenerate and vicious—Crowley who has climbed more mountains than Douglas has written articles: mountains even steeper than the epithets permissible in a Sunday newspaper article; and not so easy....

In estimating motives for the attacks on Crowley's reputation, it is helpful always to remember that he is a poet, a successful poet; that is, a poet who has tackled his poetical job successfully. The rancour of minor poets, frustrated poets, like James Douglas, is always formidable when exercised against a successful poet. It is straining the probable too far, however, to attribute all the legend of Aleister Crowley to the rancorous envy of his poetic rivals. The attack has been too vicious, even for that. We must look elsewhere, too.

The patriot Bottomley has been associated with James Douglas in the formation of the legend, or its crudest elements, in its most popular and sensational form. What shall be said of poor Bottomley? Crowley would probably say: "He has suffered enough; he has had time to think it over"—yet it will be necessary to consider Bottomley, and *John Bull*, no less than James Douglas and the *Sunday Express* as muck-throwers in chief against Aunt Sally under investigation.

For many years Crowley has lived abroad. One would have thought that sleeping dogs would be let lie; but no. *John Bull*, as recently as May 1929, described Crowley's "England's worst man," and warned him not to come to England. On arriving in London, Crowley dined pleasantly with one of the Scotland Yard chiefs, and that was that.

The publishers of this autobiography, now in the Press, have had some fun. Weird customers have walked into their offices, uttering cryptic warnings, and have vanished, leaving no traces of identity. One of the said, "Always cross your fingers when you speak to Aleister Crowley." His own fingers were crossed all the time he was in the office. He said: "That man is superman; he can read thoughts; he knows what we are thinking now." Questioned, the weird visitor would say no more, but merely withdrew, his fingers still crossed, moaning hollowly: "Remember, remember!" like the ghost of Hamlet's father.

Many other kind friends "seriously warned" the publishers, and meant well. In discussion, most of them were amazed to learn that Crowley was actually living in England, going about his business as a normal man of letters, correcting proofs, and otherwise seeing his books through the press. They were under the impress, vaguely, that he would be arrested if he set foot on these shores! Informed that Crowley had never been charged with any criminal offence in all his adventurous life, some replied: "Ah, that shows how *clever* he is!"

The legend persists.

Many booksellers refused absolutely to send out prospectuses or to handle the autobiography, even if they received orders for it. A typical objection, uttered even without an inspection of the book, was: "We don't want any of that love cult stuff here!" Practically all warned the publishers, in a genuinely friendly way, to be careful, very careful, in all dealings with Aleister Crowley.

More definitely. A stranger walked into one of the bookshops which displayed an advertisement for the book. The stranger was curiously interested in the name Aleister Crowley, and asked the bookseller many questions. He then told the following amazing story: His daughter, at a convent school in France, had been *specially warned* in lectures by a visiting priest not to read any book by Aleister Crowley. This had had the usual effect—after leaving the school she had tried to eat, or at least to gaze upon, the fruit so specifically forbidden. She had pestered her father to try and obtain some of Crowley's books for her to read!

Examples could be continued. I have quoted enough to show the wide persistence of the legend, even to the present day. The very existence of such a romantic oral tradition in this allegedly prosaic twentieth century, and while the original of the legend is still alive, is a matter of some importance at least for comparative theology; and on these grounds an inquiry should be made into its origin and development. Otherwise posterity, through its professors or modernism, will decide that Crowley was a Solar Myth. That is why I insist at the outset that he is a man; in which case the existence of the legend becomes even more interesting. If the legend is true, or even partially true; if he has killed and eaten only one coolie in the Himalayas, for example, instead of the two alleged; it will be my painful duty to bring him to justice, poet or no poet, if I can, lest he eat me. But if the legend is not true, by any chance, justice should equally be done.

II

It is axiomatic that Aleister Crowley is a man, and an extraordinary man. I think, moreover, that he is a genius. His detractors might qualify this by saying, an *evil* genius. This does not seem to me to make him less interesting as the subject of this inquiry, nor will it make him less interesting to posterity. "Evil" seems to be a question-begging epithet to apply to genius. An alternative explanation is that he is *possessed by a genius*. This seems to me to involve an occult or magical hypothesis which I cannot, in my ignorance, argue. It is essential to the legend, however, that he is or has a genius. No ordinary man could be the hero of such fables. Continued unpopularity for thirty years is not easy for a literary man to achieve. Yet Crowley has achieved it—has even consolidated his position! Bernard Shaw, once the red terror of maiden ladies in Suburbia, has become a patriarchal, almost a saintly figure. Perhaps he will be buried in Westminster Abbey, like Thomas Hardy, that other Grand Old Man, one of whose earlier books was named by critics "Jude the Obscene." Ramsay McDonald, execrated conscientious objector during he war, has become Prime Minister, no less. Other reversals of first impressions continue to prove the transitoriness of opinion. German generals and U-boat commanders are publicly welcomed to England. Aleister Crowley is not welcomed. Darwin, Huxley, Bradlaugh, and all the "atheists" are of blessed memory nowadays; but Crowley is hated and feared. Crowley is a "bad" man.

Times are changing. A new and eager generation is alleged to be resurgent after the war's horror. This generation suspects many of the traditions of its forbears. The Victorian Age, even the Edwardian Age, is not known at first hand to this generation. Mr. Gladstone is almost a myth. All the old fogies, and all the old bogies, are dying. The new and resurgent generation is amused at old-fashioned prejudices and beliefs: is rather incredulous about the pre-war days—cannot visualise them at all. But the old fogies still cling to their old bogies. Aleister Crowley is a bad man. You must cross your fingers when you speak to Aleister Crowley. He eats babies:. He worships the Devil…He is an evil genius…

Belonging, as I suppose, to the post-war generation, I take the view that all this finger-crossing and sinister whispering about a perfectly good poet, interfering with the appreciation of his poetry, is disgraceful and out to be stopped. If he is a criminal, hang him or put him in gaol, and be done with it. If he is not a criminal, let his innocence be established, somehow, so that his poetry may be read without irrelevant prejudice. If he is a religious teacher, or a religious maniac, for that matter, or a philosopher, or merely a provocative thinker, hear what he has to say, at least, before getting the jim-jams about "black magic." If he has attacked Christianity, that's no novelty! If his views upon sex are not those of St. Paul, no more are the views of many a divorce-court judge. Even if his poetry is erotic, blasphemous, indecent, obscene, corrupt, perverted, pagan, decadent, sensual, and what-not—is it good lyric? That is the question.

Posterity may regard Aleister Crowley as a great poet, or as a great, perhaps an epochal, religious teacher. I don't know, and don't care, what posterity thinks. But it is a reproach to this generation, this "emancipated" generation, that any literary man, merely because his thought is unusual, should be branded as infamous by dirty little inkslingers, propping up a pre-war bogey without troubling to inquire what damage they may do.

It is no use letting indignation go too far once this protest has been made. People of any integrity will realise that the Legend of Aleister Crowley has developed almost beyond a joke. I set myself the task of explaining precisely how the legend has arisen, in the hope that some sane appreciation of the man's work and genius may be possible. The documents appended, taken from what must be the silliest collection of press-cuttings in existence, are intended to show the part played by a section of the Press in fostering the calumny. I have gone through that collection—it is far from compete—in a detached endeavour to trace the legend's growth. Fortunately, space has necessitated many omissions, but enough are reproduced to show how a fantastic slander can grow. The position as I write two or three of its predecessors created and knew to be false.

I am far from exonerating Crowley himself. A quite extraordinary simplicity in his nature has led to systematically to invite hostility from almost every quarter, as I shall show. But in common justice he must be exonerated from the literal abominations with which he has been charged, not in the Law Courts, but in other buildings situated in Fleet Street. It is all very well to say that he should sue for libel to vindicate himself. Newspaper proprietors are invariably millionaires. Justice is free to all—who can pay for it. Crowley estimates that it would cost him at least £5,000 and probably £10,000 to fight libel actions properly against the newspapers which have defamed him. He would then have no certainty of getting a verdict, owing to the fantastic nature of the allegations made, the difficulty of disproving them because some considerable time has elapsed since the worst "exposures" were made, and the general unsavouriness, to a poet, of engaging in endless legal squabbles. It is really up to the newspaper proprietors, who will be specially asked to read this book, to make the *amende honorable* now, however late, if they are persuaded that they have piled on the infamy too thick. Of course this is a forlorn hope, but you never can tell. I pass to a consideration of the actual legend in its historical development, not sparing to blame Crowley, where Crowley is really to blame.

III

He is one of our greatest humorists, but his humour is, on the whole, unkind in its effect.

The most hapless victim of Crowley's practical joking has invariably been Crowley himself. That is, he has been the butt of his own practical jokes. Anyone familiar with his poetry will recognise that element of perversity, that subtle sense of fun, which causes him to laugh at himself in the midst of the most "serious" passages. This is maddening to sentimentalists, who were just beginning to settle down to enjoy the beauty of his thought.

"O Frater Perdurabo, how unworthy are
these sentiments!"

"D'ye want a clip on the jaw?"

Interpolations of this kind spoil the poetry, no less than his philosophical utterances, for many simple-minded readers. If W. B. Yeats had finished his Lake Isle of Innisfree with a couplet similar in sentiment to the above, he would have achieved the devastating effect which Crowley's perverse humour has upon his readers. The comparison is by no means unfair. Crowley's lyric powers are certainly not inferior to those of Yeats, his mystical thought is superior. But Yeats entirely lacks Crowley's power of self-devastation.

No writer alive is so devastating to himself, and consequently to his readers, as Aleister Crowley. If I went more deeply into this it would be to show its origin in the Oriental religions which Crowley has so intensively studied—the religious aim, for example, of achieving deep self knowledge by a breaking down of the normal intellectual self-consciousness. This inquiry would lead away from the purposes of the present study. All that need be summarised is that the fact of Crowley's perverse humour has annoyed many people, who could not see the point. His tendency to laugh unkindly at everything, and anybody, sacred and profane, including himself, has been one of the biggest contributory factors to the growth and persistence of his legend. In his search for ultimate values, for the truth beyond appearance, he has attacked anything and everybody too savagely. He has held nothing "sacred" merely because it appeared sacred. Piece by piece he has alienated that vague mass of dogma called Public Opinion, and outraged it. He has attacked, with his devastating humour, precisely those people who have no sense of humour in their doctrines.

As a Rationalist, he has attacked Christianity, particularising the most logical sects, the Plymouth Brethren and the Roman Catholics, with a vicious severity, but, on the other hand, as a mystic he has equally attacked Rationalists for their lack of imagination! Both sides detest him equally, therefore. He has hit them both on the solar plexus.

With accurate blows on the vitals, he has also enraged every possible group of vested interests in the "occult" world, particularly Theosophists, Spiritualists, Freemasons, and "Rosicrucians." His "Qabalistic" knowledge and his learnedness in every branch of occult science has made him the most formidable foe of hugger-mugger and pretentiousness in magical affairs. All the little mystics have reason to be terrified of him and his "exposures" of their camouflages. These groups, quite numerous and socially powerful, or at any rate noisy, are mainly responsible, I deduce, for the legend that he is a devil-worshipper and a practitioner of "black" magic. His attacks would not have mattered had he been as illiterate and as lacking in literary grace and logical clarity as most of his opponents.

But his excellent polemical style, the depth and breadth of his learning, the vehemence of this wit, the passionate sincerity underlying his onslaughts, have evidently been too much to be rebutted by the fair means of equivalent polemics. Capitulation or anonymous and vindictive slander were the only alternatives. The Legend grew.

Not content, however, with infuriating such specialised if powerful elements, Crowley proceeded to exercise his battering ram against every concept held cardinally by the whole Christian community: in particular by the guardians of their tradition in England, the suburbanites, the middle-class, the bourgeoisie—the "Philistines." Much of his behaviour in baiting the Philistines was, in my opinion, sheer foolishness and romantic posturing, and ought to be condemned as such, but without fingers crossed. He left Cambridge at the end of the 90s with a fortune of £40,000 to burn, and came to London. There he played the fool, admittedly, as anyone else might have done in that time, place, and circumstance. His poetry was "outrageous" in the manner of Swinburne, Baudelaire, and the Yellow Book. One of his earliest works was a poetic reply to Krafft-Ebing!

He caused his books to be printed privately with all the unction of fine paper, type and binding, at the Chiswick Press under Jacobi. Then (perhaps foolishly) he sent them out to the Press for review. He lived as "Count Svareff" in a flat in Chancery Lane, which he fitted up as a magical temple. He bought a Scottish estate at Boleskine, Iverness, and appeared at the Café Royal in full paraphernalia of a Scottish chieftain, as the "Laird of Boleskine" (sensation).

Women who remember those merry days still testify that Aleister Crowley looked enormously impressive in kilts. His legs were splendidly beautiful, probably on account of his constant mountaineering. He climbed the soft chalk of Beachy Head to the complete astonishment of the natives, no less than of experienced climbers. He began making records in Cumberland, in Wales, and on the Alps. A sinister interpretation was placed even upon these feats of agility and daring. Aleister Crowley was climbing unclimbable places. Obviously by supernatural aid. Inevitably he came to loggerheads with respectability as personified in the Alpine Club, and began exposing its members as incompetent and even as untruthful braggarts. Another hostile group! But merely in passing.

When the police in Paris refused to allow Epstein's monument to Oscar Wilde to be unveiled, because genitals were sculpted thereon, Crowley unveiled the statue by a stratagem "in the interest of art." A metal butterfly was affixed to the offending parts on the statue. Crowley removed the butterfly and wore it as a cod-piece over evening dress, triumphantly marching into the Café Royal (great sensation).

The legend grew. One would say that he was asking for notoriety, and he got it. I can think of a simpler explanation— merely in his poetic exuberance, in the fact that he really thought an artistic purpose would be served by shocking the suburbs, and in the fact that he really did not care what people thought of him, because he had enough money to be indifferent to any hostile opinion or criticism.

An injunction was taken out against him to prevent him from publishing alleged secrets of the Rosicrucians in his incredible periodical, THE EQUINOX. He appealed and won the appeal. The "secrets" were published. Resentment grew.

He gave a series of public performances of "The Rites of Eleusis" in the Caxton Hall. This brought a storm of newspaper criticism, though the performances were admitted to have been dignified in conception and execution. The legend was well away.

From time to time he "mysteriously" disappeared; to reappear eventually in his old haunts, looking years younger, refreshed in body and mind, ever more sardonic, witty, vituperative, and "wicked." On such disappearances he would walk across the Sahara, climb the Himalayas, live as a Yogi in Ceylon, walk across China, explore Mexican volcanoes, or dally in Honolulu. Such voyages are unusual, but hardly sinister, disappearances of a man from London. Yet, they, too, helped the legend along on its by now galloping way. It was said, by jaded Londoners, that Aleister Crowley had succeeded in preparing the Elixir of Life; which alone could account for his perpetual freshness and physical vitality. It was also said that he knew how to turn base metals into gold, which alone could account for his wealth, as evidenced by his sumptuously produced books, his love of good food, and his travellings. Alternately, to explain his renewals of vitality, it was suggested that he practised physical vampirism. The suggestions as to the origin of his wealth crystallized into the rumour that he obtained money from wealthy women by blackmail, intimidation, and worse.

This kind of slander invariably betrays the voice of envy and fear. As already explained the professional thaumaturges had every reason to envy Aleister Crowley's learning, and to fear his fearlessness. There was really no other possible attack upon him than the attack of malicious slander. In addition to the thaumaturgic fears, one can imagine the positive dismay of poetry reviewers, most of them, no doubt, struggling minor poets earning an odd guinea by book reviewing, on being confronted with the succession, apparently endless, of Crowley's sumptuous masterpieces! One can imagine also the rage of pasty and besotted "Bohemians" when Crowley turned up periodically, soaked in sunlight, his muscles tightened by exercise and abstinence, to be-dazzle their mistresses with his physical and mental charms. I repeat, in the literary underworld of London, there was no other available weapon against Crowley than envious, malicious slander. Unwittingly, he asked for trouble, and he got it. There was many a snake lying in the grass.

I have said that many of his actions during that Edwardian age were gratuitously foolish, that there was a lot of ninety-ish romantic bravado about his whole attitude, and his pranks. Already the reaction against Queen Victoria and what she symbolised was an established convention in advanced literary circles. Crowley, in his hot youth, went one better and made the antipathy personal to the Queen. In language which by many would be considered offensive, he described her as a fat German hausfrau; and, declaring all the Hanoverians to be usurpers, he joined the Carlist conspirators, was knighted by Don Carlos, and declared that—under the Salic Law—all Victorian knighthoods were invalid. This seems to me to have been quite a notable short cut to unpopularity in respectable English quarters, and to have been quite the wrong thing to do if his ambition was to become an idol of the middle classes. But perhaps that was not his ambition! The fact remains that in many escapades susceptible of being developed into a legend of his villainy. The bourgeois are fair game. You can insult some of the people some of the time, but there's a limit. He wrote a (probably harmless) lampoon on Queen Alexandra, printed in Paris. The whole edition was seized and destroyed by Customs officials. *Lése majesté* became incorporated in the legend. This episode again seems to me to have been more senseless than sinister.

IV

Despite all the ninetyish and Edwardian pranks just described, it could not have been said at the outbreak of the war Aleister Crowley was completely condemned by solid English opinion, whether popular in the widest sense or averagely literate. He had created a stir in professional literary and occult circles, but he had committed no widely significant public outrage. During and immediately after the war he proceeded to make good this omission. He laid himself open to three indictments, admirable for the purpose of journalistic vilifications on the million circulation scale. These three indictments were: that he was a pro-German, that he was a drug addict and trafficker, and the conducted "an abode of love" with white slave implications. In each instance Crowley himself provided just the necessary point of departure for these canards is their egregious flights.

One stands aghast at the colossal intransigeance, the complete disregard of possible results, the persistent school-boyish perverseness which could have led him to declare himself pro-German and pro-Irish during the war. I doubt if he will ever be forgiven by the English for this prank, though Bernard Shaw and Ramsay MacDonald and Bertrand Russell and Lytton Strachey have been forgiven. For as usual, Crowley took not middle course. Being by nature an active man, he could not assume the passive role of conscientious objector when their other howling demagogues took control of England, usurping sanity. When super-patriots began blackguarding the "kultur" of Wagner, Beethoven, and Nietzsche; when they howled of "atrocities" and "scraps of paper" and stampeded the English nation into hysteria for military purposes, he was indignant beyond words, as all better-class Englishmen were. Like the

ory he is at heart, he romantically had thought that
ould be conducted, from the English side at least, in
manly fashion. A victory for England by these means,
he thought, was certain, owing to moral superiority. But when
Bottomley, Lloyd George, Northcliffe and Co. took command
Crowley came to the conclusion that the ideals of England,
as thus formulated, ought *not* to triumph. In high dudgeon he
travelled to America, went in a motor boat to the Statue of
Liberty, and proclaimed the Irish Republic!

No doubt after that he felt better.

The New York Times made a three-column story of the escapade, and Crowley found himself popular with the pro-German (Irish and German) elements in New York journalism. They asked him to contribute articles to their papers, *The Fatherland* and *The International*. Willingly, Crowley complied. He is nothing if not thorough.

Now here comes the almost incredible perverseness. Landed through his impetuousness in this compromised position he proceeded to pull the leg of the serious-minded Germans as thoroughly as he had ever pulled any legs in his life! In order to parallel and parody the mad-dog British journalism, which was howling for the suppression of Santa Claus (the German), Crowley wrote a ponderous article solemnly affirming that the Kaiser was Parsifal in quest of the modern Holy Graal. This article, in all its stark irony and humour is reprinted in the present volume at page 161.

Where the joke becomes a tragedy, is that a bookseller in England was sent to gaol for three months for selling the magazine containing this very article, and that the houses of Crowley's friends in London were searched for evidences of similar treason. This deplorable incident merely increased Crowley's prestige with the pro-German elements in New York. He became *persona grata* with them, and before long he was writing practically the whole of *The International* under a dozen different names, as in the merry old days of THE EQUINOX in London. It cannot be said that *The International* under his guidance was an effective political instrument. The war seems to have steadied him. He took himself more seriously as a Magus, and an ethical teacher. He used his position as dictator of *The International*, not so much to write political articles in favour of Germany, as to expound the Law of Thelema, both explicitly and in a number of positively brilliant short stories. Even his political editorials were ethical in import. One of these, "Humanity First," he reprinted (p.157), shows fairly adequately the tendencies of his "pro-German" activities in New York.

I do not ask here that he be "forgiven" for his attitude during the way. Readers may form their own opinion, but the question should be decided on knowledge, not on hearsay.

The war steadied Crowley, to some extent—as who did it not? Even in the days of the THE EQUINOX he had been inclined to consider himself sufficiently gifted to become a religious teacher of mankind. "The Rites of Eleusis" (performed in London in 1912) had been a serious attempt to formulate a naturalistic religion, which was at the same time ceremonial; a religion to satisfy man's craving for beauty without straining his historical and scientific credulity. During his five years in America he seems to have worked out a little more fully the ethical implications of such a religion; though in this respect also his activity was not so much a new departure as an intensification of earlier thinking on the subject. When he came back to Europe in 1919 and lived in a villa which he called "The Abbey of Thelema" at Cefalù in Sicily, he seriously believed that the World War had signalised the breakdown of Christian civilisation, and that his was the tremendously responsible part of teaching an ethical code of the New Æon. It has already been remarked that Crowley never takes the middle course!

It is not my task here to expound the Law of Thelema, even if I understood it properly; but the main principle is perfectly simple in formulation—that each Individual should ascertain his True Will and do it. The new religion urges that "Every man and every woman is a star," i.e. a unit of cosmic significance and autonomy. The implications are as manifold as there are individuals in the Universe. DO WHAT THOU WILT—a command from Gods to man—is the summary of the Law which is to replace the THY WILL BE DONE—an entreaty from men to God—of earlier religions.

What matters for our present purposes is that Crowley, becoming convinced in America of the necessity of teaching this Law to Mankind, and passionately believing that his work would be of permanent value and importance to mankind, proceeded to live at Cefalù in accordance with Thelemite principles.

There is nothing particularly nefarious in this decision. I should have said he has as much right to establish a cloistered religious fraternity as, for example, the Roman Catholics. Religion, like every other form of human activity, cannot but be improved by experimental work. The first difficulty was that, Crowley's religion being naturalistic, he welcomed devotees of both sexes to his Abbey—whereas other religious institutions segregate the sexes. It was thus that he laid himself open to the ridiculous charge of establishing a "love cult" or a "free love" colony. Women, it should be noted, including Mary Magdalene, formed part of the entourage of an earlier Master, whose word was "God is Love." But this does not seem to have given rise to any pernicious "love cult" legend. When the *Sunday Express* came to vilify him for writing the DIARY OF A DRUG FIEND a morbid interest was suddenly taken in the probable sexual "goings-on" at Cefalù by critics who seemed to consider it abominable *á priori* for morbid conjecture about the sexual life in onanistic monasteries and convents—or in thousands of other villas in Italy and on the Riviera!

He was "hard-up" at this time. His fortune was now exhausted. Even had he wished to swank in London, as in the dear days departed, he no longer had the means, in ready cash at least. (So much, by the way, for the legend of German gold—though that allegation, like its modern counterpart in Russian gold—is a bogy which barely raises a smile, even, nowadays.) It was the intention of earning what is commonly called an honest living by the pen that he came to London in 1922 and contracted to write the DIARY OF A DRUG FIEND.

I mention the fact of his privation at this time because there is a moral in it somewhere. It is not that pride goeth before a fall, as the vindictive might suppose; or that a young man with £40,000 should invest in Consols and never touch the principal, instead of spending his capital exploring far countries, performing elaborate magical rituals, dining and wining well, and printing fine editions of his poetry. The moral is, look out for the worst attacks from your enemies. It was at this moment that all the steady resentment against Aleister Crowley, a thunderstorm that had been brewing in literary and occult coteries in London for many years, burst with the violence of a typhoon upon him.

Two incidents brought matters to a head—the publication of THE DIARY OF A DRUG FIEND, and the unfortunate death of Raoul

Loveday at Cefalù. James Douglas and the editor of *John Bull* perceived in these events their opportunity for an orgy of that sensational vituperative journalism of which they are probably the world's champions. Nothing like the vindictiveness of these attacks upon Crowley has ever been known in history of English journalism. If only as a record of this phase of literature in the 20th century, the extracts from these articles quoted herein deserve preservation for posterity in a form more permanent than on the crumbling sawdust of the newspaper page.

What is so tragic about the episode is, that at the outset of his first serious campaign to propagate an ethical code, at the moment when he had, as it were, steadied down to this serious purpose, when he had no longer any desire or intention to shock the suburbs, Aleister Crowley found himself presented to millions of horrified readers as a creature of degradation and villainy hitherto unexampled in the history of mankind! I find this tragic irony not without its perverse, almost Crowleyan, humour. And I think also that now, after more than seven years, the joke has gone far enough....

The DIARY OF A DRUG FIEND is a novel which was written by Crowley in twenty-seven days in order to raise money from the honest employments of his literary talent. It is a novel, a work of fiction. It paints with the skill of a masterly psychologist, with toxicological learning not at all surprising in one who had studied so thoroughly the esoteric, and with the descriptive power of a practiced writer, all the horrors and degradations of the vice of drug taking—at that time and now, a vice alleged to be prevalent amongst the stupidly idle classes of bourgeois "society." The book shows how the habit may be cured by self-discipline and a training of the will according to the principles of Thelema. It seems evident on analysis that Crowley wished to take an extreme example of moral disintegration in order to show the possibilities of Thelema.

The book was withdrawn after its third thousand by Messrs. Collins, who ought to have known better. They were helped to this decision by one of the shrillest and most hysterical denunciations of a book ever written, even by such a journalist as James Douglas.

It is impossible to estimate how much underground scurrility this incident has added to the Crowley legend. If the book had not been withdrawn from the market people would have been able to form their own opinion of its merits. But as it happened, the general public had to take for granted the denunciations which alone they read, and to make horrified conjectures themselves as to the nature of its contents. It was supposed, for example, by people who could not obtain the book, that Crowley himself was a Drug Fiend, and that this was his personal diary: The legend even developed to the rumour still current that Crowley is the head of a secret and international Order which controls the manufacture and sale of illicit drugs throughout the world—that the "Magical Order of Initiates" was nothing else than a camouflaged drug-running society! Poor Crowley! Literally poor Crowley, who had written that hasty novel in order to make sure of his commissariat at Cefalù! The tables were indeed turned at last upon that harumscarum of the pre-war days who published occult "secrets" in THE EQUINOX.

Even in THE DRUG FIEND incident, it will be noted, I do not totally exonerate Aleister Crowley from my principal indictment of him in these pages—for innocence or carelessness of results which may follow from misinterpretation by his readers of whatever serious message his literary works contain;

his over-estimation of the amount of critical intelligence in the world. In my view the novel shows all the defects of its hasty composition. It also shows all the attractive qualities of poetic imagination, which are undeniably Crowley's. On balance, it is a novel well worth reading. But at this time, and in those circumstances, it was the worst possible tactics, considered propaganda for the Law of Thelema. It is almost the biggest blunder that he could have made. It was literally a deliverance into the hands of James Douglas. One would say almost that he unconsciously wished to frustrate himself as a religious teacher of mankind: that his Yoga-practice of literary self-annihilation had achieved its apotheosis.

THE DIARY OF A DRUG FIEND was a colossal mistake in judgment, I repeat, and he cannot be held completely blameless, however much we sympathise with him, for the distortions of Douglas and Bottomley's successors which followed.

Quite otherwise is the sad incident of Raoul Loveday's death at Cefalù, which occurred as a climax of Crowley's own misfortunes. It should be fairly obvious that Crowley was in no way responsible, directly or indirectly, for this tragedy. In her recently published book the widow, Betty May Loveday, declares that her husband died of enteric fever following the drinking of unfiltered water, despite the fact that Crowley had distinctly warned all the members of the household against drinking such water. She adds that Loveday had proper medical supervision, and that everything possible was done by Crowley in the circumstances. We must leave it at that. How the *Sunday Express* and *John Bull* made a sensational campaign against Crowley will be shown in due course. Meanwhile it is enough to remark that, when the day came that *John Bull* could print a full page article about Aleister Crowley under a headline, unprecedented in the history of abuse, of "A Man We'd Like to Hang"; when Crowley, who is, after all, human and a sensitive creature, could find himself virtually accused of the murder of one of his dearest and closest friends—when this catastrophic slander could overwhelm a fine poet and idealist at a time of deprivation and, as it happened, illness, I insist emphatically that the silly jokes of destiny had been carried too far: that the hitherto comparatively harmless "Legend of Aleister Crowley" had developed in malice and vindictiveness beyond the permissible limits of decency and taste, even on the standards of the crudest sensational journalism.

John Bull subsequently apologised for insinuating that Loveday had been a drug-addict in the Abbey of Cefalù. But that one small apology could never overtake the great galloping defamations of Crowley which had preceded it.

The *Sunday Express* has never apologised. James Douglas, the protestant pope, is infallible.

In what follows I have tried to present the documents pertaining to the "Legend" of Aleister Crowley in order that the reader may arrive at an informed opinion as to its origin and development. He is a man, and an interesting man. He is a poet, and an interesting poet; and where so much subterranean rumour is in circulation no harm can be done to anybody guiltless by letting a little daylight into the dark places.

THE EARLY PERIOD, 1896-1907

CHAPTER II

The Early Period, 1896-1907

Aleister Crowley was born in 1875, educated privately, and at Malvern; and entered Trinity College, Cambridge, in 1895. During his youth and adolescence his chief hobbies had been poetry, chemistry, mathematics and chess; his chief sport had been rock climbing, in which he had already attained a notable proficiency; and his chief antipathies had been religion, as practised among the strict Plymouth Brethren to which his family belonged, and home life as personified in the bigotry and fantastically repressive Puritanism of his mother. It was his mother who called him "The Beast 666," a mystical designation which he has not been averse from accepting.

At Cambridge he read assiduously, but without much relation to the prescribed courses, intending to be entered for the Diplomatic Service. He seems to have abandoned this career for a singularly undiplomatic life as a poet, magician and explorer. While at Cambridge his first poetical works ACELDAMA and WHITE STAINS were published. These were followed immediately by THE TALE OF ARCHAIS, SONGS OF THE SPIRIT, and JEPHTHAH, all published in 1898, at the end of which year he went down from Cambridge.

Ten years after the publication of his first work, he had issued no less than thirty volumes, mostly of poetry, the full bibliography of which it is impossible at this date to set in order, as most were issued privately in small editions. The publication of his COLLECTED WORKS in three volumes, 1905-6-7, marks the end of the "Early Period," as does the appearance of a work in criticism and praise of his poetry, entitled The Star in the West, by Captain (now Col.) J.F. C. Fuller in 1907.

It was at the end of this period, and in appreciation of Captain Fuller's book, that Florence Farr Emery was moved to utter the following strangely prophetic words:

> It is a hydra-headed monster, this London Opinion, but we should not be surprised at all to see an almost unparalleled event, namely, every one of those hydra-heads moving with a single purpose, and that the denunciation of Mr. Aleister Crowley and all his works.
>
> Now this would be a remarkable achievement for a young gentleman who only left Cambridge quite a few years ago. It requires a certain amount of serious purpose to stir Public Opinion into active opposition, and the only question is, has Mr. Crowley a serious purpose?... A final judgment is that the young man is a remarkable product of an unremarkable age.... His power of expression is extraordinary; his kite flies, but he never fails to jerk it back to earth with some touch of ridicule or bathos which makes it still an open question whether he will excite that life-giving animosity on the part of Public Opinion which is only accorded to the most dangerous thinkers. (*New Age*, 1907).

In order to prove that Mrs. Emery's astonishment at Crowley at this date was not based merely upon his literary fecundity, it is only necessary to add that during this ten years, at intervals while engaged in the composition of the thirty publications previously mentioned, he had made, amongst other explorations, a trip entirely round the world (1900-02) via New York, Mexico, San Francisco, Honolulu, Japan, China and Ceylon; including in his itinerary an expedition of six months to the Himalayas with the Chogo Ri (K2) expedition of 1902, spending sixty-five days on the Baltoro Glacier, and attaining a height of 22,000 feet.

He had also studied and practised the Hindu spiritual discipline of Yoga (Ceylon, 1901), bought an estate in Scotland at Boleskine, Inverness, married the sister of Gerald Kelly (1903), travelled to Cairo (1904), revisited Ceylon for big game shooting (1904), taken part in the expedition to Kangchenjunga (1905) which reached the height of approximately 23,000 feet, travelled down the Irrawaddy to Rangoon, walked across China (1906) and visited Morocco with the Earl of Tankerville (1907).

One gets from a short recital of these activities an impression of the adventurous and energetic character of the man, who was truly "a remarkable product of an unremarkable age." His file of Press cuttings for this period is self-evidently incomplete. His early poetry seems to have had, at the hands of reviewers, the usual pontifical reception which a young poet has to expect. He came scarcely at all before the notice of that wider public interested in the sensational. Only once, in his skirmish with G. K. Chesterton, was there anything like an attempt at serious appreciation or controversy. The impression which remains after going through these Press criticisms of his early poetry, is that Crowley was recognised to be a poet of distinction, whose ideas nevertheless were possibly dangerous, though the reviewers could not be sure. Even after thirty volumes, though the reviewers had probably not seen more than a few of these, the Press, if not over-sympathetic, was definitely not more hostile than is usual with poets. The fireworks were to come later.

UNDERGRADUATE VERSE (1896-7)

WHITE STAINS and ACELDAMA were not sent to the Press for review. The former, an undergraduate "poetic reply to Krafft-Ebing," was very privately printed and circulated. One review of Aceldama remains on record, a copy having presumably made its way into the editorial sanctums of the *Cantab*.

> Induced by we know not what course of reading, the book is not one that can be recommended to the young, for though its stanzas are sufficiently musical, there runs through them a vein of scepticism and licentiousness which requires to be treated with caution.

It is amusing to notice that this very first appearance of Crowley as an object of criticism, even in the undergraduate Press of his contemporaries at Cambridge, contains a "warning" against him which foreshadows the vulgar attacks of later years. The Cambridge undergraduate journals, as it happens, never sponsored Crowley very kindly. A short time after going down he published IN RESIDENCE, a collection of undergraduate lyrics, which was received by the *Granta* with the following unkind salutation:

> Oh, Crowley, name for future fame!
> (Do you pronounce it Croully?)

> Whate'er the worth of this your mirth
>   It reads a trifle foully.
> Cast before swine these pearls of thine,
>   O, great Aleister Crowley
> "Granta" to-day, not strange to say,
>   Repudiates them wholly.

THE TALE OF ARCHAIS (1898), another undergraduate effort, was described in the *Cambridge Review* as "spurious romantised mythology"; though in the *Cambridge Magazine* an enthusiast declared that "the author holds the first place among latter-day poets." Amusingly enough the *Oxford Magazine* was rather impressed by this Cambridge poet, remarking that "his song runs clear and free from the pollution of sensuality."(!) The literary papers in London had little to say, as might be expected. The *Academy* noted "a certain command of facile rhythm." the *Saturday Review* discovered a "pleasant vein of fancy," but thought the poem "utterly lacked originality."

SONGS OF THE SPIRIT was more widely noticed. The *Manchester Guardian* was quite sympathetic:

> A little book of unusual quality.... We have read it with admiration for its intense spirituality, as well as for its technical superiority, and with sympathy for its spontaneous reflection of certain moods that Mr. Crowley pursues with an utterance at once mysterious and vivid. ...The verse is free from obvious artifice and eccentricity, it is fiery and clear-measured and easy of phrasing.... The glowing imagery seizes and holds fast the vagueness of shifting impressions.

The *Athenaum* was nasty:

> Difficult to read, and where they touch definite things, more sensual than sensuous. We cannot say that these verses deserve to be read.

The *Church Times*, heedless of history's censure for encouraging one who was to become a formidable antagonist, issued a benediction:

> Ambitious verse, which, if we are right in supposing it to be the work of youth, enables us to predict excellent work from Mr. Crowley when his philosophy of life has been matured.

Even the *Granta*, under a stately moral reserve, did not disdain to encourage the young poet:

> Though we cannot identify ourselves with the sentiments expressed in its pages, we must acknowledge that the poems show very considerable literary merit.

And the *Literary Gazette* spoke with heavy common sense:

> There is too much of the cant of a contest between earthly and heavenly love in his pages.... A book of wandering cries such as this we cannot regard as of much significance.... We would advise him to be less introspective.

JEPHTHAH (1898)

At the end of 1898 JEPHTHAH was published and apparently sent out for review in the usual manner. It was taken quite seriously as giving promise of good things to come. The critics seem to have enjoyed their opportunity to teach a young poet his business. The following extracts are characteristic:

Church Times: —

Not mere immaturity, but absolute rawness; all the intolerant dogmatism of the undergraduate conjoined with the unconvincing passionateness of a somewhat belated disciple of Swinburne.... Mr. Crowley takes himself too seriously; it is the manner of precocious youth. He is not competent to settle all human problems with a lyric....

Vanity Fair: —

We cannot say that there is no promise in the book. At present it is all a rushing and rioting of words with the vicious scorn of all the world that the young love. But age and experience may do much, and Mr. Crowley may write good poetry some day.... Bathos and banality! but the writer may improve.

Manchester Guardian: —

If Mr. Swinburne had never written, we should all be hailing Mr. Aleister Crowley as a very great poet indeed. Jephthah is a largely conceived and finely executed piece of work which alone is enough to prove Mr. Crowley's independent claim to the name of poet. It will be easier to judge his orbit when he gets a little further away from the giant planet that has drawn him.

The Scotsman: —

It is a work of no small power, the choral lyrics reaching remarkable heights and more than compensating for the rather obscure theology with which the piece as a whole is clouded.... There are many fine sonnets and pieces that carry one on by their rush of impetuous feeling and musical language.... The thought is worthy, never deep or simple, and the verse turns out to be a sort of serpentine dance with coloured lights of feeling thrown on from the outside.

Literary World:—

If at times wanting in taste, Mr. Crowley has at least indubitable singing power, and mastery of form. We look with interest for his next work.

Morning Post:—

Melodious and eloquent, but it does not bear analysis and it reads more like a parody than real poetry.... We gather from intrinsic evidence that the author is young; and when he has sown literary wild oats he may possibly become a great poet.

Aberdeen Journal:—

He has caught the spirit in the style of Swinburne, and in some respects the pupil is greater than his master. If occasionally his meaning is incomprehensible, it is certainly not often that he lapses into meaningless verbiage, and his worst sins in this respect could be without difficulty paralleled from Swinburne and Browning. Mr. Crowley has a vivid imagination and the true poetical temperament. The most captious critic will find very little to blame in the smooth, majestic flow of his rhythms. He has handled his material with consummate skill.... And we confidently anticipate that Mr. Aleister Crowley will in no long time take his place as an English poet of acknowledged eminence.

Other papers joined in deploring his youth, and, at the same time, encouraged his future. The *Birmingham Gazette* sums up:

...From the power and earnestness of the book before us, we are inclined to favour his chances of the future.

From Sydney, New South Wales, came an Antipodean echo:

The high level touched at times is not always maintained, but some of the songs are classical in their mournful melody. Mr. Crowley will be heard of more favourably yet, if he will but rein in that prancing Pegasus of his.—*Sydney Morning Herald.*

The *Pall Mall Gazette* alone expressed a positive desire for the poet to shut up his shop:

Mr. Crowley takes himself very seriously; he believes he has a mission, he thinks there is at least a probability that his poetry will make a stir in the world and among posterity. We wish we could think so too... but we are compelled to forego this pleasant prospect and to state our opinion that this poet's estimate of his own powers is not at all likely to be shared by a large number of his fellow men. We gather that Mr. Crowley is a young man.... The signs of youth are present throughout the volume. There is the customary homage to Mr. Swinburne, and (alas!) the usual failure to write in his manner without adopting his mannerisms.... We do not wish to dwell unfavourably upon youthful affectations.... We would not have devoted so much space to Mr. Crowley had not some of the press criticisms of his previous publication shown us that a certain number of our contemporaries were at one time disposed to encourage him to persist in his metrical exercises....

Most honest of all, perhaps, was the *Jewish World*:

We confess to having experienced the utmost difficulty in determining the merit and meaning of Mr. Crowley's work.... His talent is undeniable, but wholly misused in a vain quest after the incomprehensible.

THE MOTHER'S TRAGEDY (1901)

By the time these fatherly reviews had appeared Crowley was in far countries, thinking of many other things, from Mexican volcanoes to Himalayan avalanches. Nevertheless, a privately printed edition of a new poem, THE MOTHER'S TRAGEDY, appeared in 1901, keeping interest awake in his absence. The book was discussed with vigor in the coteries. Again, Cambridge attacked him and Oxford defended him:

Cambridge Review:—

Invidious as it may seem to deal hardly with a privately printed book, courteously sent for review, this volume demands an emphatic protest from all lovers of literature and decency. Dedicated by as much as is comprehensible of the prologue to the suggestive exposition of the obscene, it never deviates for one moment from its appointed task. If, however, to the clean-minded man the book is revolting, to the artist it is a monstrosity. Such thoughts as may lurk between its covers are, fortunately, concealed in such a maze of intricate verbiage, that it is only here and there that we catch a glimpse of the horrors that lie behind.

Oxford Magazine:—

Mr. Crowley has a claim to recognition as a true poet. Most men who have thought deeply on life's problems recognise that the current religion of nearly all their fellow men is an idle mockery.... Mr. Crowley seems to hold that the world is reeking with rottenness—and he is, to a great extent, right.... These daring verses contain a large share of elemental truth. But we live in a hypocritical age, and apparently the author of these extraordinary poems realises the fact, for his volume is privately printed.... Magnificent poems—pagan in their intensity and vividness of colouring.

Probably the same Cambridge undergraduate, or one of his friends, damned the book unequivocally in the *Athenaum*:

> Mr. Aleister Crowley is a kind of middle-class Swinburne at second hand, without the scholarship, without the splendid phrase, without the ardour of beauty. He has a certain rhythmical fluency, and in that statement all his literary merits are summed up. If the reader can form a conception of a wind-bag foaming at the mouth, he will get some notion of "The Mother's Tragedy." and other Poems (privately printed). Even this mixed metaphor will not convey to him the morbid unpleasantness of Mr. Crowley's taste in subjects. "The Mother's Tragedy" is a drama of incest, crudely and violently treated. Some of the shorter poems are worse.

At the same time a rather kindly appreciation occurred in the *Academy*:

> It is not long since we reviewed a book by Mr. Aleister Crowley, and mingled blame with praise, like "Crusty Christopher." So we must still do; for "The

Mother's Tragedy" treads too hard on the heels of his previous volume for any modification of the qualities we then noted. There is the old vigour and boldness, the sinewy phrase that takes you by the throat (as it were) and throttles the praise out of you; but also it is unkempt, wild, shattering in form, unskillful in coherent expression, profuse in awkward and misleading constructions as of old. For many of these poems there is no word but powerful; yet it is (we might almost say) the power of insanity, so little is it under the author's own control, so contorted and spasmodic is it, proceeding by vehement leaps and rushes of speech, abruptly checked by thick and struggling utterance. Often admirable in forceful felicity, it is equally often exasperating by its choked and imperfect expression. Withal there is thought; it is turbid with meaning, only too turbid at many times. Yet this is a fault on the right side. We would rather wrestle with Mr. Crowley's obscurity (and he is often densely, faultily obscure, through trying to say more in a line than he has the gift to say) than wade through the tepid vacuity of most minor verse. The poem only too manifestly reveals its own effort.... Yet its sheer power constantly makes way through the dead weight of its defects; while it is throughout grave and dignified. The poet always knows what he is saying, though the reader may often desperately wish that *he* did.... Mr. Crowley, we may add, frequently expresses things with all his uncompromising completeness, which poetry (to our minds) had better leave unexpressed.

THE SOUL OF OSIRIS (1901)

In 1901, too, Kegan Paul published THE SOUL OF OSIRIS. The usual contradictory reviews appeared. One critic wrote:

> The power...which is undeniable, cannot hide from us either its extreme unpleasantness or the gratuitously offensive treatment.... There is a wearisome occurrence of all the ugly machinery with which the fleshly school of poetry has made us too familiar.

A copy reached New York, causing an enthusiast to remark, in the *New York Nation*:

> The depth and volume and the passionate intensity of the feeling in many of these poems are unmistakable, as are the frequent richness and visionary splendour of the imagery and the aptness and the transfiguring power of the rhythms.

and a discovery was made in Plymouth:

> We are compelled to read even where the subject matter fails to attract, and we venture to think that in Aleister Crowley we have found a poet, whose genius has yet to unfold.... *(Western Morning News, Plymouth.)*

G. K. Chesterton, himself beginning to sparkle at that time, perceived an opportunity to exercise both his own religious predelections and his capacity for merry paradox, in an important article in the *Daily News*, which is quoted extensively hereunder, together with a reply subsequently published by Crowley as a note to THE SWORD OF SONG:

SOUL OF OSIRIS

Article by G. K. Chesterton.   *Daily News.*
June 18th, 1901.

To the side of a mind concerned with idle merriment there is certainly something a little funny in Mr. Crowley's passionate deities who bear such names as Mout, and Nuit, and Ra, and Shu, and Hormakhu. They do not seem to the English mind to lend themselves to pious exhilaration. Mr. Crowley says in the same poem:

> "The burden is too hard to bear;
>   I took too adamant a cross;
> This sackcloth rends my soul to wear
>   My self-denial is as dross.
> O, Shu, that holdest up the sky,
>   Hold up thy servant, lest he die!"

We have all possible respect for Mr. Crowley's religious symbols and we do not object to his calling upon Shu at any hour of the night. Only it would be unreasonable of him to complain if his religious exercises were generally mistaken for an effort to drive away cats.

Moreover, the poets of Mr. Crowley's school have, among all their merits, some genuine intellectual dangers from this tendency to import religious, this free-trade in Gods. That all creeds are significant and all Gods divine we willingly agree. But this is rather a reason for being content with our own than for attempting to steal other people's. The affectation in many modern mystics of adopting an Oriental civilisation and mode of thought must cause much harmless merriment among actual Orientals. The notion that a turban and a few vows will make an Englishman a Hindu is quite on a par with the idea that a black hat and an Oxford degree will make a Hindu an Englishman. We wonder whether our Buddhistic philosophers have ever read a florid letter in Baboo English. We suspect that the said type of document, is in reality exceedingly like the philosophic essays written by Englishmen about the splendours of Eastern thought. Sometimes European mystics deserve something worse than mere laughter at the hands of Orientals. If ever was person whom honest Hindus would have been justified in tearing to pieces it was Madame Blavatsky.

That our world-worn men of art should believe for a moment that moral salvation is possible and supremely important is an unmixed benefit.... If Mr. Crowley and the new mystics think for one moment that an Egyptian desert is more mystic than an English meadow, that a palm tree is more poetic than a Sussex beech, that a broken temple of Osiris is more supernatural than a Baptist Chapel in Brixton, then they are sectarians.... But Mr. Crowley is a strong and genuine poet, and we have little doubt that he will work up from his appreciation of the Temple of Osiris to that loftier and wider work of the human imagination, the appreciation of the Brixton Chapel.

To this Crowley replied, in a note to "The Sword of Song":

> I must take the opportunity to protest against the charge brought by Mr. Chesterton against the Englishmen "who write philosophical essays on the splendour of Eastern thought."
>
> If he confines his strictures to the translators of that well-known Eastern work the "Old Testament" I am with him; any modern Biblical critic will tell him what I mean. It took a long time, too, for the missionaries (and Tommy Atkins) to discover that "Budd" was not a "great Gawd." But then they did not want to, and in any case sympathy and intelligence are not precisely the most salient qualities in either soldiers or missionaries. But nothing is more absurd than to compare men like Sir W. Jones, Sir R. Burton, Von Hammer-Purgstall, Sir E. Arnold, Prof. Max Muller, Me, Prof. Rhyas Davids, Lane and the rest of the illustrious Orientalists to the poor and ignorant Hindus whose letters occasionally delight the readers of the Sporting Times, such letters being usually written by public scribes for a few pice in the native bazaar. As to "Babs" (Babu, I may mention, is the equivalent to our "mister," and not the name of a savage tribe), Mr. Chesterton, from his Brixton Brahmaloka, may look forth and see that the "Babu" cannot understand Western ideas; but a distinguished civil servant in the Madras Presidency, second wrangler in a very good year, assured me that he had met a native

whose mathematical knowledge was superior to that of the average senior wrangler, and that he had met several others who approached that standard. His specific attack on Madame Blavatsky is equally unjust, as many natives, not theosophists, have spoken to me of her in the highest terms. "Honest Hindus" cannot be expected to think as Mr. Chesterton deems likely, as he is unfortunately himself a Western, and in the same quagmire of misapprehension as Prof. Max Mullet and the Rest. Madame Blavatsky's work was to remind the Hindus of the excellence of their own shastras, to show that some Westerns held identical ideas, and thus countermine the dishonest representations of the missionaries. I am sufficiently well known as a bitter opponent of "Theosophy" to risk nothing in making these remarks.

I trust that the sense of public duty which inspires these strictures will not be taken as incompatible with the gratitude I owe to him for his exceedingly kind and dispassionate review of my "Soul of Osiris."

I would counsel him, however, to leave alone the Brixton Chapel, and to "work up from his appreciation of the 'Soul of Osiris' to that loftier and wider work of the human imagination, the appreciation of the *Sporting Times*!

Mr. Chesterton thinks it funny that I should call upon "Shu." Has he forgotten that the Christian God may be most suitably invoked by the name "Yah"? I should be sorry if God were to mistake his religious enthusiasms for the derisive ribaldry of the London "gamin." Similar remarks apply to "El" and other Hebrai-Christian deities.

TANNHAUSER (1902)

Crowley returned to Europe at the end of 1902, naturally with a number of works for publication. He had written TANNHAUSER in Mexico, and had sent it Kegan Paul for publication. It appeared before his return from the Himalayas, and seems to have been altogether too much for the professional literateurs. The following attempts at criticism are typical:

Pall Mall Gazette:—

Such magnificence of paper, print, and margin, that we trust we are right in assuming that he is possessed of material wealth even greater than the wealth of languages, which he displays so profusely throughout the volume. With all these attractions, he nevertheless fails to stir us at all deeply.

Daily Chronicle:—

We are not sure that Mr. Aleister Crowley treats life as a sacrament, because we do not understand him.

AHAB

Nothing daunted, he proceeded to have AHAB printed in original Caxton type which gave the critics a simple excuse to declare themselves puzzled:

Manchester Guardian:—

Mr. Aleister Crowley's previous work has been eccentric, and at the best he has done more to provoke curiosity than to give confidence. Now he chooses to handicap himself by printing his poems in a type that must inevitable impose restrictions upon many readers.

Glasgow Herald:—

Mr. Aleister Crowley, not content with the usual risk of the neglect that threatens minor poets, has had his verse set up in what is apparently German black-letter, thereby tempting the most conscientious reviewer to take his volume as read.

THE STAR AND THE GARTER

Puzzlement increased with the publication in the same year of THE STAR AND THE GARTER, a poem which combines elements of the lampoon with profound metaphysics and simple "naughtiness." the provincial Press gave a naïve expression to the general bewilderment:

Bath Chronicle:—
A peculiar dissertation on love.

Arbroath Herald:—
So clever that one finds some of it utterly unintelligible.

Liverpool Courier:—
Even when understanding lags behind we read with pleasure.

ALICE, AN ADULTERY

This book at least was more intelligible. In a series of sonnets, the poet describes faithfully and lyrically an adultery in Honolulu, day by day, for the fifty days it lasted. The final parting is described as follows:

> "So the last kiss passed like a poison-pain,
> Knowing we might not ever kiss again.
> Mad tears fell fast: 'Next year!' in cruel distress
> We sobbed, and stretched our arms out, and despaired,
> And—parted. Out the brute-side of truth flared;
> Thank God I've finished with that foolishness!"

The work was published by the Society for the Propagation of Religious Truth at Boleskine, Inverness, which cause the *Glasgow Herald* to remark:

> We confess to being so dense as to miss the essentially religious purpose of the book.... But the power of many of the sonnets is undeniable.... For the perfect art of the lyrics, for their tender music, we have nothing but admiration....

Pious horror smote some moralist writing for the *Daily News*:

> He has a good deal of talent of a weak, neurotic, lyrical kind, but is purely derivative.... For matter, the author has turned to some unsavoury reminiscences of a change acquaintance, reminiscences which plead to be forgotten, and which none but the very shameless would dare to put into print.... Most of the book is in need of what a poet has called "the purging fire." One or two single lines are good. One or two stanzas have a meaningless derivative prettiness....

But in the *English Review*, then in its hey-day, some lover of poetry was moved to the following careful piece of criticism:

> These love songs of his have a wonderful ardour, and almost Sapphic fury. They flash and shine with images that are like little streaks of flame.... The verse with which the book opens has all the hard brilliance and the lustre which are characteristic of the writer's work. The opening picture breaks on the senses like a shaft of sudden sunshine.... Among many things that occur to one in reading Mr. Crowley's verses is their singular disseverance from the things of the day, their entire lack of what is called "The Modern Note" in poetry. We must think that he deliberately shut his eyes to the writings of the intimate, romantic, impressionist school, or how else could so susceptible an artist have escaped its infection?
>
> Another thing that is apparent is the fitfulness of his inspiration. A journey through the garden of the poet's verses has all the excitement and the drawbacks of making one's way by means of illumination of lightning. There is a lot of darkness to a small proportion of extreme brilliance, though, perhaps, as with all rare and superfine things this is necessarily the case.
>
> For the rest: great metrical force, rhythms so violent as almost sometimes to exhaust themselves, and, in some of the later work, a curious employment in his philosophy of paradox....

THE SWORD OF SONG

This book is the outstanding work of Crowley's early period. Its outward appearance is startling. Five hundred copies only were printed. The book was a large quarto, printed in red and black throughout. The binding was in navy blue, with a gold design on the front, consisting of the number "666" thrice repeated in the form of a square. On the back cover, in gold, the name Aleister Crowley appears transliterated into Hebrew characters, arranged in the form of a square to add up to 666. The number of pages excluding introduction was 194, of which 62 pages contain the poems Ascension Day and Pentecost, with headlines and marginal notes and occasional single lines rubricated. The remainder of the book, 132 pages, consists of notes on the poems and appendices, the latter mainly an exposition and criticism of Buddhist philosophy. It may be that posterity will consider this book amongst the greatest of Crowley's works. His contemporaries certainly had little or no opportunity of appreciating it. The few copies printed, though issued at the incredibly low price of 10*s*., could scarcely have been other than a slow leaven. However, a few copies reached the Press. G. K. Chesterton again took up his controversy with Crowley, printing a three column review of the book in the *Daily News* under the title Mr. Crowley and the Creeds. To this Crowley replied in a pamphlet entitled A Child of Ephraim:

THE SWORD OF SONG
Daily News, Sept., 1904.

Mr. Aleister Crowley has always been, in my opinion, a good poet; his "Soul of Osiris," written during an Egyptian mood, was better poetry than this Browningesque rhapsody in a Buddhist mood; but this also, though very affected, is very interesting. But the main fact about it is that it is the expression of a man who has really found Buddhism more satisfactory than Christianity.

Mr. Crowley begins his poem, I believe, with an earnest intention to explain the beauty of the Buddhist philosophy; he knows a great deal about it; he believes in it. But as he went on writing, one thing became stronger and stronger in his soul—the living hatred of Christianity.... Mr. Crowley has got something into his soul stronger even the beautiful passion of the man who believes in Buddhism; he has the passion of the man who does not believe in Christianity. He adds one more testimony to the endless series of testimonies to the fascination and vitality of the faith.... A casual carpenter wanders about a string of villages, and suddenly a horde of rich men and sceptics and Sadducees and respectable persons rushed at him and nailed him up like vermin; then people saw that he was a god. He had proved that he was not a common man, for he was murdered. And ever since his creed has proved that it is not a common hypothesis, for it is hatred.

Next week I hope to make a fully study of Mr. Crowley's interpretation of Buddhism, for I have not room for it in this column to-day.

G. K. Chesterton.

Crowley's reply was as follows:

Our Author's main argument for the Christian religion is that it is hatred. To bring me as a witness to this colossal enthymeme he has the sublime courage to state that my "Sword of Song" begins with an effort to expound Buddhism, but that my hatred of Christianity overcame me as I went on, and that I end up literally raving. My book is possibly difficult in many ways, but only Mr. Chesterton would have tried to understand it by reading it backward.

It is surely an ascertainable fact that, while the first 29 pages are almost exclusively occupied with an attack of Christianity as bitter and violent as I can make it, the remaining 161 are composed of *(a)* an attack on materialism; *(b)* an essay on metaphysics opposing Advaitism; *(c)* an attempt to demonstrate the close analogy between the canonical Buddhist doctrine and that of modern Agnostics. None of these deal with Christianity at all, save for a chance and casual word. I look forward with pleasure to a new History of England, in which it will be pointed out how the warlike enthusiasm aroused by the Tibetan expedition led to the disastrous plunge into the Boer War; disastrous because the separation of the Transvaal which resulted therefrom left us so weak that we fell as easy prey to William the Conqueror....

But to the enthymeme itself. A word is enough to expose it. Other things have been hated before and since Christ lived,—if he lived. Slavery was hatred. Does Our Logician argue therefore the vitality of slavery? Does the fact that a cobra is alive prove it to be innocuous?....

With the reported murder of Jesus of Nazareth I am not concerned. Surely Our Fid. Def. will find little support in his claim on half of death. We all die. The two thieves were "nailed up like vermin" on either side of Christ by precisely the same people; are they also Gods? To found a religion on the fact of death, murder though it were, is hardly more than African fetichism. Does death prove more than life? Will Mr. Chesterton never be happy until he is hanged?....!

Postscript.—On the appearance of his article "Mr. Crowley and the Creeds" I signified my intention to reply. It aborted his attack of me, and he has not since been heard of.

In the midst of the words he was trying to say,
In the midst of his laughter and glee,
He has softly and suddenly vanished away—
I suppose I always was a bit of a Boojum!

It is worth recalling that only 500 copies of the book were printed. Obviously the public could form no first-hand opinion of the merits of the book. People who managed to view a copy were perhaps more astonished by the external eccentricities of the work than by its undoubtedly serious religious import. The poetry itself, to say the least, is spectacular. Some of it was written on the Baltoro Glacier, while Crowley was recovering from malaria(!) at a height of over 22,000 feet. In parts it is distinctly colloquial, e.g.,

"No Yogi shot his Chandra so.
Will Christ return? What ho? What ho!"

Frequently the poet is baldly sceptical:
"The metaphysics of these verses
Is perfectly absurd. My curse is
No sooner in an iron word
I formulate my thought than I
Perceive the same to be absurd."

At times the rhyming virtuosity is breath-taking. Immured in his snow-covered tent, with a copy of Browning's Collected Works by his side, the poet was able to amuse himself, between chess games, by finding rhymes for such words as "refuge," "reverence," "country," "virgin," "courtesan," "Euripides," "Aristophanes," "Æschylus," "Aischulos," "Sophocles," "Aristobulos," "Alcibiades," "fortress," "unfashionable," "sandwich." "perorate," "silver," "bishop" "(eight rimes for this word), "Sidney" (three rimes for this), "maniac," "Leviticus," "Cornelius," "Abramelin," "Brahmacharya," "Kismet," "Winchester," "Christ Church," "Worship." "Chesterton," "Srotapatti," "Balliol," etc.

The marginal notes are provocative:

What is truth? said jesting Pilate: but Crowley waits for an answer."
Buddha rebukes Poet.
Poet defies his uncle.
Sporting offer!
Who pardons Judas?
Creator in Heaven suffers Hell's pangs, owing to reproaches of bard.
Jesus dismissed with a jest.
How clever I am!
Crowley dismissed with a jest.
Bard checkmates himself.
Bard is pleased with himself.
Some poetry.
Pontius Pilate as a Surrey magistrate.

The footnotes are equally provocative, e.g.:

Eton.—A school, noted for its breed of cads. The Battle of Waterloo (1815) was won on its playing fields.

Christ Ascends.—And I tell you frankly that if he does not come back by the time I have finished reading these proofs, I shall give him up.

The full title of the work is
> THE SWORD OF SONG
> CALLED BY CHRISTIANS
> THE BOOK OF THE BEAST

He refers in the text to those who, taking a hint from his mother,
> By all sorts of monkey tricks
> Add up my name to six six six.

and, as one accepting destiny, he boasts
> Ho! I adopt the number. Look
> At the quaint wrapper of this book!
> I will deserve it if I can:
> It is the number of a Man.

It only remains to add that, at publication, copies were sent to all living persons mentioned in the book, accompanied by the following circular letter:

> Letters and Telegrams: Boleskine Foyers is sufficient address.
>
> Bills, Writs, Summonses, etc.: Camp XI, The Baltoro Glacier, Baltistan.

O Millionaire!	My lord Marquis,
Mr. Editor!	My lord Viscount,
Dear Mrs. Eddy	My lord Earl,
Your Holiness the Pope!	My lord,
Your Imperial Majesty!	Reverend Sir,
Your Royal Highness!	Sir,
Dear Miss Corelli,	Fellow,
Your Serene Highness!	Dog!,
My lord Cardinal	Mr. Congressman,

My lord Archbishop,   Mr. Senator,
My lord Duke,   Mr. President,
  (or the feminine of any of these), as shown by underlining it,
Courtesy demands, in view of the
  (*a*) tribute to your genius
  (*b*) attack on your (*1*) political
              (*2*) moral
              (*3*) social
              (*4*) mental
              (*5*) physical character
  (*c*) homage to your grandeur
  (*d*) reference to your conduct
  (*e*) appeal to your better feelings
on page   of my masterpiece, "The Sword of Song," that I should send you a copy, as I do herewith, to give you an opportunity of defending yourself against my monstrous assertions, thanking me for the advertisement, or—in short, replying as may best seem to you to suit the case.

              Your humble, obedient servant,
                   ALEISTER CROWLEY.

Probably no book of Crowley's so completely reveals the complexity and perverseness of his character. A copy seems to have reached a contributor of the *Yorkshire Post*, who commented:

> Mr. Crowley's poetry, if such it may be called, is not serious, at any rate, in its form. It is more colloquia than the Ingoldsby Legends, and his matter, or rather his way of expressing it, is distinctly, though quite needlessly, calculated to irritate not only the Christians

to whom it is directed address, but even every serious-minded man of any religion whatsoever.... And yet Mr. Crowley's book shows wide reading. If the form and tone of his work prevent his being read, Mr. Crowley will only have himself to thank.

Another contributor, to *St. James's Gazette*, summed up as follows:

> A jumble of cheap profanity, with clever handling of metre and rhyme. Christianity will survive—but the author's reputation may not be so fortunate.

The rationalist *Literary Guide* adequately expressed the bewilderment of all readers who were able to obtain the book:

> "The Sword of Song" is a masterpiece of learning and satire. In light and quaint or graceful verse all philosophical systems are discussed and dismissed. The second part of the book, written in prose, deals with possible means of research, so that we may progress from the unsatisfactory state of the sceptic to a real knowledge, founded on scientific method and basis, of the spiritual facts of the Universe.
>
> It is not easy to review Mr. Crowley. One of the most brilliant of contemporary writers.... Mr. Crowley's short poems in particular reveal the possession of a beautiful and genuine vein of poetry, which, like the precious metals, is at times scarcely discernible among the rugged quartz in which it is embedded. With a true poetic feeling allied to remarkable learning, and with a pretty wit of his own, Mr. Crowley is well equipped for producing a work of permanent value.... Good work may be found in "The Sword of Song," but there

is even more which will arouse in the average reader (to whom, however, Mr. Crowley obviously does not appeal) no other feelings than one of sheer bewilderment. Sometimes an oasis of beauty will reveal the author's power to charm, the good-humoured egotism will tickle the fancy, the quaint allusiveness of the notes will raise the eyelid of wonder.... With regard to the prose portions of the volume, the essay on "Science and Buddhism" reveals some penetrating touches; but we have to confess that the discourse on "Ontology" baffles our comprehension. The poetical epilogue is beautiful and interesting.

Why Jesus Wept

Only 500 copies of this dramatic poem were printed. The work was written in Ceylon, and is a satire on English society, dedicated to Mr. G. K. Chesterton, amongst others, including Christ and the poet's unborn child. Mr. Chesterton appears as a person in the drama, as a deity presiding at a meeting of Plymouth Brethren:

> Above, with an olive branch in one hand and a copy of the *Daily News* in the other, floats Mr. G. K. Chesterton in the position Padmasana [the "lotus" position, in which Buddha is commonly represented as sitting—*footnote*], singing "Beneath the Cross of Jesus" with one voice, and attempting "God Save the Queen!" with the other in a fashion calculated to turn any marine, if but he be filled with honourable ambition to excel in the traditional exploits of his corps, green with envy.

When one of the Brethren mentions "The Baptist minister at Brixton" there is a stage direction (*"Mr. Chesterton executes the cake walk"*), Crowley thereby accepting a challenge made to him by Chesterton in the review of the SOUL OF OSIRIS.

Only one review seems to have appeared of this book, which is, by the way, far from blasphemous in any intelligent sense of the term, and is really an expression, very vivid, of a poet's sensitive hatred of all the shams and cruelties of a prurient pseudo-Christian society: summed up in the epilogue:

> I say what I have seen ill-done
> In honest clean lived Albion;
> ....
> Still, since de *gustibus non est*—
> (My schoolboy readers know the rest!
> I much prefer—that is, mere I —
> Solitude to Society.
> And that is why I sit and spoil
> So much clean paper with such toil
> By Kandy Lake in far Ceylon.
> I have my old pyjamas on:
> I shake my soles from Britain's dust:
> I shall not go there till I must;
> And when I must—ah, you suppose
> Even I must!—I hold my nose.
> Farewell, you filthy-minded people!
> I know a stable from a steeple.
> Farewell, my decent-minded friend!
> I know arc lights from candle-ends.
> Farewell! A poet begs your alms,
> Will walk awhile among the palms.
> An honest love, a loyal kiss,
> Can show him better worlds than this;
> Nor will he come again to yours
> While he knows champak stars from sewers.

The poem was too much even for the supposedly "emancipated" *Literary Guide* which commented:

> It is a work which, as far as pious innocence is concerned, should be kept strictly under lock and key.... The strange mingling of ribaldry, indecency, poetry, and wit, could be perpetrated by no one but Mr. Crowley; and certainly no other author would issue, under his own name, such a ruthless violation of conventionalities. The display of Mr. Crowley's rampant virility does not always take a commendable turn, and many readers will regret that his genius has been given so loose a range.

OTHER EARLY WORKS

These included THE ARGONAUTS (1904), ORACLES, ORPHEUS AND ROSA MUNDI (1905), and GARGOYLES 1906. The following reviews of the ARGONAUTS will serve as a summary of Press opinion of his work at this period:

Literary Wold:—

> We have read from the beginning to the end, sometimes with amazement, sometimes with amusement, sometimes with admiration. We are puzzled to know how it comes to pass that a writer capable of what is best in the "Argonauts" can possibly put into print what is worst. ...It is a great pity that Mr. Aleister Crowley's muse is so capricious..

Manchester Guardian:—

> Beginning with a feeling of prejudice, we are soon beguiled into genuine interest.... The admirable thing is the author's skill as a craftsman in verse. In blank

verse he shows an easy and assured grace of style, and the lyrical portions are distinguished by exquisite metrical beauty. ...In spite of his oddities, he possesses a real and rare poetical gift.

THE STAR IN THE WEST

In 1905 Crowley was again in the Himalayas, on the Kangchenjunga expedition. In 1906, he was engaged in a walk across China, accompanied by his wife and child; in 1907 he was sojourning among the desert tribes of Morocco, with the Earl of Tankerville as a companion. During these three years, his COLLECTED WORKS appeared in three india-paper volumes, one each year. Simultaneously, an "Essay Competition" was announced in a circular issued by the Society for the Propagation of Religious Truth (Boleskine), headed as follows:

> The Chance of the Year!
> The Chance of the Century!
> The Chance of the Geologic Period!!!

The circular offered a prize of £100 for an essay on the works of Aleister Crowley. The COLLECTED WORKS were offered to bona fide competitors for the sum of 5*s*. each volume, a bargain price indubitably. Naturally the Press perceived a good opportunity for sarcasm at the expense of the "Society for the Propagation of Religious Truth." The *Manchester Courier*:

> This method of propagating minor poetry is not more remarkable than the publication of such poetry by the Society.

Nevertheless, one notable competitor entered for, and eventually won, this strange competition—Capt. J. F. C. Fuller of the Oxfordshire Light Infantry, and now (1930) at the War

Office. His winning essay was published separately in 1907 under the title of THE STAR IN THE WEST. To say the least, it is as unusual a work of criticism as has ever been written about any poet in any place in time. There was not question of "damning with faint praise." The gallant Captain's prose style thunders like a regiment of cavalry in full charge:

> It has taken 100,000,000 years to produce Aleister Crowley. The world has indeed laboured, and has at last brought forth a man....Crowley has twisted a subtle cord, on which he has suspended the universe, and swinging it round has sent the whole fickle world conception of these excogitating spiders into those realms which lie behind Time and beyond Space. He stands on the virgin rock of Pyrrhonic-Zoroastrianism, which unlike the Hindu world-conception, stands on neither Elephant nor Tortoise, but on the Absolute Zero of the metaphysical Qabalists.
>
> The question now is, what is Crowleyanity or Pyrrhonic-Zoroastrianism? and the answer is as follows:
>
> "Hosanna to the Son of David! Blessed is He that cometh in the name of the Lord. Hosanna in the highest!" For this day there has been born in Albion a greater than David Hume, and a more illustrious than David Hume, even had he been genuine.
>
> And he shall be called "Immanuel," that is "God with us," or being interpreted Aleister Crowley, the spiritual son of Immanuel whose surname was Cant!
>
> Again:
>
> From the silver goblet of laughter, that leaden cup of weeping, have the nations drunk the dregs of many

lives; for the woman arrayed in purple and scarlet, and decked with pearls and precious stones, hath made them drunk on the golden cup of her abominations, on the wine of her fornications, on the filthy philtres of her whoredoms; and they have become truculent, and boisterous, and mad; cloaking the silken nakedness of the day with their woolen shroud of darkness, and seeking in the depths of night the mysteries of everlasting light.

O Dweller in the Land of Uz, thou also shalt be made drunken, but thy cup shall be hewn from the sapphire of the heavens, and thy wine shall be crushed from the clusters of innumerable stars; and thou shalt make thyself naked, and thy white limbs shall be splashed with the purple foam of immortality. Thou shalt tear the jewelled tassels from the purse of thy spendthrift Fancy, and shalt scatter to the winds the gold and silver coins of thy thrifty Imagination; and the wine of thy Folly shalt thou shower midst the braided locks of laughing comets, and the glittering cup of thine Illusions shalt thou hurl beyond the confines of Space over the very rim of Time.

Thou O seeker after Wisdom, and Virtue, and multiscient Truth, thou O wanderer in the groves of Eleusis, thou, even thou shalt drink of the wine of Iacchus, and thy cup shall be as a triple flame set with sapphire, and beryl, and amethyst; for it is the cup of the Adepts, and of Heroes, and of Gods. Then all the absinthial bitterness of thine heart shall vanish midst the chaunting of souls lost in the ocean of understanding for ever and everlasting.

After two more paragraphs in this vein, the chapter from which this excerpt is taken ends as follows:

O wine of Iacchus, O wine, wine, wine.

I am far from alleging that the whole of Captain Fuller's book sustains the rhetoric of the excerpts quoted. Most of his pages are concerned with what might be called a straightforward account of Aleister Crowley's poetic and philosophical achievements. THE STAR IN THE WEST will always be readable, if only for the extensive quotations of lyrics from Crowley's own works which glitter in its pages. The philosophical exposition of "Crowleyanity" is often pedantically elementary; and like most expositions of a philosopher's thought, is not at all to be preferred to the original it expounds.

At the same time, viewing Captain Fuller's work in retrospect, one cannot but feel that his reaction to Crowley's poetry had been a most spontaneous and passionately sincere gesture, which only a very gallant man could have had the courage to make. Very few military officers, one presumes, would have the courage, greater than that required in "Seeking the bubble reputation even in the cannon's mouth," to accept and acclaim publicly a poet such as Crowley in terms such as those used by Captain J. F. C. Fuller. THE STAR IN THE WEST, over-enthusiastically written as it was, was a brave book. Deep had called to deep. Two manly men, an explorer and a soldier, were now conjoined in an effort to acclaim Ecstasy, Dionysian ecstasy, as a poetic and human goal—for the English! In a desert of stolidity, dullness, and puritan timidity, this mountain torrent suddenly began thundering. However, the desert soaked up the torrent, and remained a desert.

I repeat. In 1907 Aleister Crowley, with Captain Fuller as aide de camp, could have formulated a way out for the English from the complete moral, poetical, and spiritual sloth into which the nation had degenerated since the days of its high Elizabethan glory. It was Crowley who wrote:

> We are the poets! We are the children of wood and stream, of mist and mountain, of sun and wind! We adore the moon and the stars, and go into the London streets at midnight seeking Their kisses as our birthright. We are the Greeks—and God grant ye all, my brothers, to be as happy in your loves! and to us the rites of Eleusis should open the door of Heaven, and we shall enter and see God face to face.
>
> * * * * *
>
> Under the stars I go forth, my brothers, and drink of that lustral dew; I will return, my brothers, when I have seen God face to face, and read within those eternal eyes the secret that shall make you free.
>
> Then will I choose you and test you and instruct you in the Mysteries of Eleusis, oh ye brave hearts, and cool eyes, and trembling lips! I will put a live coal upon your lips, and flowers upon your eyes, and a sword in your hearts, and ye also shall see God face to face.
>
> Thus shall we give back its youth to the world, for like tongues of triple flame we shall brood upon the Great Deep—Hail unto the Lords of the Groves of Eleusis!

The "test" failed, or appeared to fail—for the whole of history is not yet written. It is no matter for surprise, now that the Victorian Age, and even the Edwardian Age, is fading in the memory of the Oldest Inhabitants; now that we are able to realise what damage nineteenth century commercialism really did to poetry, that Florence Farr could have expected all the hydra-heads of Public Opinion to move with the single purpose of denouncing Aleister Crowley and all his works. He was indeed too remarkable for that unremarkable age. Not a product of the age, but potentially its scourge. Like Daniel, Captain Fuller had seen mystically a Writing on the Wall; but he could not make the English Belshazzars see that vision.

A true commentary upon the relation of Aleister Crowley as Poet to his public at his time is contained in a naive criticism of THE STAR IN THE WEST, which appeared in the *Daily Chronicle* in 1907:

> Here is a master voice in song, and none the less masterly because of its being unknown. It has rarely fallen to the lot of man to be the author of 32 books, ranging in prices from two guineas to half a crown each, and to have a book of 327 pages written about his work, and still be an unknown voice in the land. In this fact alone there is a certain kind of distinction, the greatness that comes of being rare. Such is Aleister Crowley.

"EQUINOX" PERIOD, 1908-1914

CHAPTER III

The "Equinox" Period, 1908-1914

If we remember that Aleister Crowley is a poet, both in his work and in his life, and that his preoccupation with "Magick" during the days of the famous Equinox was a fulfilment of his promise, previously quoted, to "give back its youth to the world," we shall understand better what happened during his "Equinox Period." Until 1907, his poetry had been mainly poetical, that is not *technically* concerned with Magick as such. To this statement there are of course exceptions. The GOETIA OF SOLOMON THE KING, definitely a technical treatise on Magick, had been published as early as 1904. Two years earlier he had published an elucidation of the Tarot entitled AMBROSII MAGI HORTUS ROSARUM. There is also some technical exposition of Magick in THE SWORD OF SONG. Nevertheless his numerous publications could be described more generally as poetry than as Magick; perhaps a kind of *practical* poetry. Most of his writings during this period show a preoccupation, much more marked than previously, with what is loosely termed the "occult."

The EQUINOX appeared in ten volumes, two a year, at the vernal and autumnal equinoxes, from 1909 to 1913. There has never been anything at all comparable to it in the history of English literary journalism. "It may be hazarded roundly," said

Mr. Harold Monro in the *Poetry Review*, "that the whole of the EQUINOX is a creation of the amazing Mr. Crowley. His antics are as wild as the devil's, he dances through its pages like a mad magician. It is a sort of enchanted variety entertainment. I cannot discover when it is not serious."

This is a very fair statement of the reception which might have been expected for the EQUINOX in "cultured" literary circles. There were, however, other less disinterested parties for whom the EQUINOX was little short of a nightmare. The professional occultists were first startled, and then terrified by its brilliancy, violence, and ruthlessness in exposing their inadequacies. Legal action was resorted to in order to restrain it, if possible. This failing, a campaign of unparalleled scurrility was initiated apropos of ceremonial public performances of the "Rites of Eleusis." Meanwhile contemptuously ignoring distractions, "the amazing Mr. Crowley" continued to bring out the EQUINOX, portly volume after portly volume, all beautifully printed and bound in white and gold, transcending any possible criticism, beyond all normal categories, whether literary or occult.

KONX OM PAX

In the summer of 1908 Crowley went for a walk across the wilder parts of Spain, accompanied by the young poet Victor B. Neuburg. His physical energy in all its abundance of virility seems to have positively required these strenuous expressions. Nevertheless, his publications were not in abeyance. In that same year appeared KONX OM PAX, a series of "Essays in Light," consisting of a short story, a dramatic skit, a philosophic essay, and a collection of lyrics. A stanza from the Dedication may be quoted:

> St. Paul spoke up on the Hill of Mars
>   To the empty headed Athenians;
> But I would rather talk to the stars
>   Than to empty headed Athenians.
> It's only too easy to form a cult,
>   To cry crusade with "Deus Vult" —
> But you won't get much of a good result
>   From empty headed Athenians.

Less concretely, the author forestalled possible criticism:

> The light wherein I write is not of reason; it is not the darkness of unreason; it is the LVX of that which, first mastering and then transcending the reason, illumines all the darkness caused by the interference of the opposite waves of thought...by overleaping their limitations. A thing is not necessarily A or not A. It is absurd to say of Virtue that it is Green or not Green; for virtue has nothing to do with colour. It is one of the most suggestive definitions of KONX — the LVX of the Brethren of the Rosy Cross — that it transcends all these possible pairs of opposites. Nor does this sound nonsensical to those who are acquainted with that LVX. But to those who do not, it must (I fear) remain as obscure and ridiculous as spherical trigonometry to the inhabitants of Flatland.

Despite this postulated transcendence of academic logic, the book remains and will remain one of the most "readable" of Crowley's works. Five hundred copies were printed, and the book is utterly unobtainable nowadays. Apart from whatever may be its serious purpose, it may be readily classified as a piece of exquisite humorous literature, to say the least. Even

John Bell enjoyed the jokes, not having, apparently, at that time lost his sense of humour:

> The author is evidently that rare combination of genius — a humorist and a philosopher.... I was moved to so much laughter that I barely escaped a convulsion.

The *Literary Guide*, beginning, no doubt, to be more afraid of Crowley than of the legitimate antagonists of the Rationalist Press Association, spoke under a strange reserve:

> Verbal fireworks. A wild and wasteful heterogeneous collection of weird words.... Still, one cannot but admire the author's oftimes skilful jugglery with words and his kaleidoscopically changing humour, even though one deplores his prodigality.

The *Scotsman* was disconcerted:

> This disconcerting volume of nebulous disquisitions in amorphous prose, relieved at intervals by verses which are formally musical, but substantially inconsequential and inane.... A rambling miscellany which along with much quizzing and much nonsense, vaguely reflects some of the ideas of the day.... More tolerable in its verse than in its prose, for a poet is not expected to be sensible. Readers who are already acquainted with the writings of Mr. Aleister Crowley need not be told that his imagination disport itself in a manner calculated to stun the middle classes.

A junior reporter on the *Perthshire Courier* grappled in vain with the problem of Crowley, and justified his opening description of the "Athenians."

What can one really say about a production such as this? The first question one is disposed to ask is: What is it all about? At best it looks like one big sneer at the Christian faith. There is a great deal that is undoubtedly smart and clever, revealing at times real genius, but presented in such a chaotic mystic rigmarole that the reader must needs stop his ears.... There is some marvellous verse, but there is more in it to deplore than to admire. We cannot conceive how a man with the culture of Mr. Crowley could sit down and write and see put into print some of the stanzas. This is essentially a top shelf book, not suitable for all.

LIBER 777

It is difficult to see how Crowley could have had time to prepare this impressive Dictionary of Comparative Religions. The *Occult Review* declared that it contains as much information as many an intelligent reader at the Museum has been able to collect in years. This book, too, is unobtainable nowadays, and is much sought after by students of the "Qabalistic" systems. The work is thus described by the writer in the *Occult Review*:

...This work has only to come under the notice of the right people to be sure of a ready sale. In its author's words, it represents "an attempt to systematize alike the date of mysticism and the results of comparative religion," and so far as any book can succeed in such an attempt, this book does succeed; that is to say, it condenses in some sixty pages as much information as many an intelligent reader at the Museum has been able to collect in years. The book proper consists of a table of "Correspondences," and is, in fact, an attempt to reduce to a common denominator the symbolism of as many religious and magical systems as the author is acquainted with...

The Cabalistic information is very full, and there are tables of Egyptian and Hindu deities, as well as of colours, perfumes, plants, stones, and animals. The information concerning the tarot and geomancy exceeds that to be found in some treatises devoted exclusively to those subjects. The author appears to be acquainted with Chinese, Arabic, and other classic texts. Here your reviewer in unable to follow him but his Hebrew does credit alike to him and his printer.... Much that has been jealously and foolishly kept secret in the past is here.

The *Buddhist Review*, however, did not take kindly to the work:

No Buddhist would consider it worth while to pass from the crystalline clearness of his own religion to this involved obscurity. Some of the language is extremely undignified.

THE EQUINOX APPEARS

In the same year appeared the first two volumes of Crowley's prodigious periodical, of which Frank Harris wrote in *Vanity Fair*:

The EQUINOX is permanent in its stately size and type, continuous in it periodical character, permanent—in the value of its contents.

The anti-thaumaturgic thaumaturges of the Rationalist Press Association were unequivocally hostile in the *Literary Guide*:

> Expensively printed lunacy, astrology, etc., in oriental occidental jargon.

The editor of *Light*, official Spiritualist organ, was seriously perturbed, and feared the worst in a ponderous editorial:

A DIAKKA PUBLICATION

> It easily takes rank as the most vigorous swearer and blasphemous in respectable modern literature. Moreover its swearing and blasphemy are splendidly done, with immense style and glorious colouring. Its contributors certainly know how to write, though occasionally they remind one of certain efforts that have emanated from lunatic asylums where gorgeousness of imagination and riotous language are by no means unknown. But underneath all, there is a huge wealth of knowledge, a few indications of serious feeling, and a big flow of occult thought. Yet with all its "illuminism" it is so much of a mocker that we have before us the figure of a Mephistopheles.... The Equinox is put forth with a certain pomp, its writers are by no means negligible in competence. All we say is that they remind us of Diakkas and Jingles, and occasionally of Colney Hatch.... The reference to black mass and the chaotic mixture may possibly help to explain the rumours of devil worship which were persistent not long ago. Perhaps we have here the key to that dark door...

The point of view of the "man in the street," or in other words of the paragraphists of the daily papers, was presented by, for example, the *Morning Leader*:

> A mysterious publication called "The Equinox," the official organ of the A.˙.A.˙. has just released upon a long-suffering world.... It is a sort of thing no fellow can understand. One gathers vaguely out of the confusion that it deals with such things as Magic, wizardry, mysticism, and so on; but what the special line is, remains a baffling mystery.... From frequent references to some people called the Brothers of the A.˙.A.˙. one gathers that they have a lot to do with this weird venture; but a grim perusal of an article purporting to explain the Order...leaves one without any real clue as to their identity. True, the Chief of the Brothers is definitely named, his name being "V.V.V.V.V." but five V's or even six V's, do not strike one as being a name likely to be well known at any local post office.... One gets all kinds of entertainments in "The Equinox"...Poetry gets a strong show, but it is uncomfortable reading....

The second number contains the first installment of what was to become a sensational "exposure" of the rituals of a quasi-secret society known as the Hermetic Order of the Golden Dawn. The "Neophyte" ritual was published at great length, with fifty-four diagrams illustrative of the mysteries. A further series of "revelations" was promised. Consternation overwhelmed the members of the Golden Dawn.

During this year, it should be mentioned in passing, Crowley undertook an expedition to the Sahara, accompanied by V. B. Neuburg. The latter, with Captain Fuller, had become intimately associated with the detailed work of producing the Equinox.

MATHERS vs. CROWLEY

EQUINOX No. 3 was due to be published on March 21st, 1910. Ten days before this date Crowley was served with a writ of summons, issued on behalf of S. L. Mathers, which claimed an injunction

> Restraining the defendant, his servants, and agents from printing, publishing, or causing to be printed or published in the third number of the book or magazine known as the EQUINOX or otherwise disclosing any matter relating to the secrets, forms, rituals, or transactions of a certain order known as the Rosicrucian Order, of which the plaintiff was the Chief or Head. (*Times Law Reports*.)

On March 14th, Mathers obtained *ex parte* an interim injunction to restrain Crowley, as proprietor and editor of the EQUINOX, from publishing the secret rituals and ceremonies of the Rosicrucian Order; stating in his affidavit that he was the Chief or Head of that Order, and that the exclusive copyright of the rituals, ceremonies, and manuscripts of the Order were vested in him, he being founder and compiler of them. The injunction was granted on March 18th.

On March 21st, the day of the equinox, Crowley appealed before Lord Justice Williams, Lord Justice Moulton, and Lord Justice Farwell. The Court allowed his appeal, and the EQUINOX duly appeared at the Equinox.

The case was widely reported in the Press as a principal "news story." There had been much laughter in Court, particularly when the affidavit of Mathers was read; and when counsel passed up to their Lordships a copy of the EQUINOX, drawing their attention to the following paragraph (written by Capt. Fuller):

Obsessed by the chimera of his mind, locked in the labyrinth of his imagination, Man wanders on through the shadowy dream land he himself has begotten.... Slave to his own tyranny, shrieking under his own lash, the higher he builds the gloomy walls of his prison, the louder he howls for liberty.... If he is a ploughman he wants more fields to till; if a physician more bodies to cure; if a priest, more souls to save; if a soldier more countries to conquer; *if a lawyer, more wretches to hang*....

Counsel for Mathers urged at one point that irreparable injury would be done "because the cat will be out of the bag." Lord Justice Williams remarked: "a great deal of the cat came out of the bad in September (laughter)." Lord Justice Farwell added: "And I think it is a dead cat (laughter)."

Together with full reports of the action, the Press further "revealed" the secrets of the Rosicrucians, copying them from the liberated Equinox. The whole episode was a definite win for Crowley, and one presumes that the frustrated Brethren of the Golden Dawn gnashed their teeth impotently and bided their time.

More Books of Poetry

The year 1910 was full of incident. In addition to the publication of Nos. 3 and 4 of the Equinox, Crowley arranged a series of ceremonial performances of the Rites of Eleusis at Caxton Hall in October-November. These were attacked in the sensational Press in terms which led to the libel action of early 1911, which will be described later. Meanwhile, he published three impressive and beautifully printed volumes of poetry, The Winged Beetle, Ambergris, and The Bagh-I-Muattar.

Of the WINGED BEETLE, an excited writer in the *Occult Review* declaimed as follows:

> In the face of the whole horde of reviewers, critics, and in the face of the British public, I declare that Aleister Crowley is among the first of living English poets. It will not be many years before this fact is generally recognised and duly appreciated.... What is not least remarkable is his amazing variety.... The range of his subjects is almost infinite...his poems are ablaze with the white heat of ecstasy, the passionate desire of the Overman towards his ultimate consummation, reunion with God.

AMBERGRIS was, on the whole, well reviewed, the *Nation* paying him the compliment of passionate sincerity:

> Precisely what species of mysticism he professes, we need not stop to determine. Its importance to him is immense; it is the hinge of his whole thought. To us, its importance is simply that it carries him often into excellent poetry.... A very casual glance will convince anyone with understanding eyes that Mr. Crowley is as passionately possessed by his theme as any poet has ever been. This should ensure a constant achievement of notable poetry.

In a long critical article published in the Australian papers, the poet and critic, A. G. Stephens, made a handsome tribute:

> Accept Crowley or refuse him, he brings his own atmosphere and captivates you, and finally captures: there is such a tide of life in him. He is not "minor" because he has a pulse and a strong opinion; he does not flutter,

he soars. Soars best when closest earth: his abstractions are empty: he needs the living model to inspire his art. ...All readers of verse know that there is ear-poetry and eye-poetry. Crowley makes an usual appeal both to eye and ear. His ivory shapes go singing themselves golden tunes.... Crowley writes shapes, beautiful shapes, beautiful coloured shapes like chryselephantine statuettes. His still with lines and rhymes, words and phrases, is more than a craft.

While a writer in the ENGLISH REVIEW made an interesting commentary:

> A certain perverseness or wilfulness is manifest in much of his work.... He has been roundly condemned, treated to impertinence, and in some cases extravagantly praised, but no one seems to have given him that deadly kind of appreciation which is the lazy critic's heartfelt thanks that there is nothing to criticize. Nobody has called him a classical poet....

Criticism of the EQUINOX at this period are as might be expected:

> The new number of "The Equinox" continues to keep up the tradition of the earlier numbers as to size, the mystical nature of its contents, and the unintelligibility of many of the articles.... (*Review of Reviews*.)

> Here is the weirdest muddle that one could well stumble across in this most muddled age.... Powerfully individualistic, descending sometimes nearly to the level of the sordid, soaring sometimes nearly to the heights of genius, the matter could not be reviewed properly in twenty times the space that we can give it.... Those

who are certain of their sanity and the breadth of their viewpoint should read this magazine when they get the opportunity. Theosophists will find the few references to Theosophy anything but complimentary.... (*Theosophy in Scotland.*)

THE RITES OF ELEUSIS PERFORMED

As an Epilogue to his COLLECTED WORKS, 1907, Crowley had written an essay, ELEUSIS, in which occurs the following paragraph:

> We need not be surprised to see as we do that religion is dead in London; here it demands no greater sacrifice than that of an hour's leisure in the week, and even, offers to replace that with social consideration for the old, and opportunities of flirtation for the young.

Again, in ORPHEUS (1905), he had written the rapturous Dionysian chant which begins:

> I bring ye wine from above,
>   From the vats of the storied sun;
> For every one of ye love,
>   And life for every one.
> Ye shall dance on hill and level;
>   Ye shall sing in hollows and height
> In the festal mystical revel,
>   The rapturous Bacchanal rite!
> The rocks and trees are yours,
>   And the waters under the hill,
> By the might of that which endures,
>   The holy heaven of will!

The essay Eleusis is a passionate statement of the necessity for revitalising religion:

> Better get forty shillings or a month than live and die as lived and died John Bright!
>
> Better be a Shaker, or a camp-meeting homunculus, or a Chatauqua girl, or a Keswick week lunatic, or an Evan Roberts revivalist, or even a common maniac, than a smug Evangelical banker's clerk with a greasy wife and three gifted children—to be bank clerks after him!
>
> Better be a flagellant, or one who dances as David danced before the Lord, than a bishop who is universally respected, even by the boys he used to baste when he was headmaster of a great English public school!
>
> That is, if religion is your aim, if you are spiritually minded; if you interpret every phenomenon that is presented to your sensorium as a particular dealing of God with your soul.
>
> But if come back from the celebration of the Eucharist and say, "Mr. Hogwash was very dull today," you will never get to heaven, where the good poets live, and nobody else; nor to hell, whose inhabitants are exclusively bad poets.

The essay concludes, as already quoted:

> Then will I choose you and test you and instruct you in the mysteries of Eleusis.... Thus shall we give back its youth to the world....

It was doubtless in continuance of this essentially religious and true purpose that Crowley wrote, early in 1910, an Invocation to Luna in the form of a poetical ritual; and further, performed the Invocation ceremonially, the violinist Leila

Waddell and Victor Neuberg assisting him. They had considerable success, as is testified by the following description, contributed to the *Sketch* by Raymond Radclyffe, a financial journalist, quite sceptical of "Magick" as such, who was present on one occasion. It is necessary to quote this article fully, in view of the attacks upon Crowley which were to follow in other quarters:

> *The Sketch.*   *August 24, 1910.*
> ### A NEW RELIGION
>
> A certain number of literary people know the name of Aleister Crowley as a poet. A few regard him as a magician. But a small and select circle revere him as the hierophant of a new religion. This creed Captain Fuller, in a book on the subject extending to 327 pages, calls "Crowleyanity." I do not pretend to know what Captain Fuller means. He is deeply read in philosophy, and the takes Crowley very seriously. I do not quite see whither Crowley himself is driving; but I imagine that the main idea in the brain of this remarkable poet is to plant Eastern Transcendental Buddhism, which attains its ultimate end in Samadhi, in English soil under the guise of Ceremonial Magic.
>
> Possibly the average human being requires and desires ceremony. Even the simplest Methodist uses some sort of ceremony, and Crowley, who is quite in earnest in his endeavor to attain such unusual conditions of mind as are called ecstasy, believes that the gateway to Ecstasy can be reached through Ceremonial Magic. He has saturated himself with the magic of the East—a very real thing, in tune with the Eastern mind. He is

well read in the modern metaphysicians, all of whom have attempted to explain the unexplainable.

He abandons these. They appeal only to the brain, and once their jargon is mastered they lead nowhere; least of all to Ecstasy! He goes back upon ceremony, because he thinks that it helps the mind to get outside itself. He declares that if you repeat an invocation solemnly and aloud, "expectant of some great and mysterious result" you will experience a deep sense of spiritual communion.

He is now holding a series of seances.

I attended at the offices of the Equinox. I climbed the interminable stairs. I was received by a gentleman robed in white carrying a drawn sword.

The room was dark; only a dull-red light shone upon an altar. Various young men, picturesquely clad in robes of white, red, or black, stood at different points round the room. Some held swords. The incense made a haze, through which I saw a small white statue, illuminated by a tiny lamp hung high on the cornice.

A brother recited "the banishing ritual of the Pentagram" impressively and with due earnestness. Another brother was commanded to "purify the Temple with water." This was done. Then, we witnessed the "Consecration of the Temple with Fire," whereupon Crowley, habited in black, and accompanied by the brethren, led "the Mystic Circumambulation." They walked round the altar twice or thrice in a sort of religious procession. Gradually, one by one, those of the company who were mere onlookers were beckoned into the circle. The Master of the Ceremonies then ordered a brother to "bear the Cup of Libation." The brother went round the room, offering each a large golden bowl full of some pleasant-smelling drink. We drank in turn. This over, a stalwart brother strode into the centre and proclaimed "The Twelvefold Certitude of God." Artemis was then invoked by the greater ritual of the Hexagram. More Libation. Aleister Crowley read us the Song of Orpheus from the Argonauts.

Following upon this song we drank our third Libation, and then the brothers led into the room a draped figure, masked in that curious blue tint we mentally associated with Hecate. The lady, for it was a lady, was enthroned on a seat high above Crowley himself. By this time the ceremony had grown weird and impressive, and its influence was increased when the poet recited in solemn and reverent voice Swinburne's glorious first chorus from "Atalanta" that begins "When the hounds of Sprint." Again a Libation; again an invocation to Artemis. After further ceremonies, Frater Omnia Vincam was commanded to dance "the dance of Syrinx and Pan in honour of our lady Artemis. A young poet, whose verse is often read, astonished me by a graceful and beautiful dance, which he continued until he fell exhausted in the middle of the room, where, by the way, he lay until the end. Crowley then made supplication to the goddess in a beautiful and unpublished poem. A dead silence ensued. After a long pause, the figure enthroned took a violin and played—played with passion and feeling, like a master. We were thrilled to our very bones. Once again the figure took the violin and played an Abend Lied so beautifully, so gracefully, and with such intense feeling that in very deed most of us experienced that Ecstasy which Crowley so earnestly seeks. Then came a prolonged and intense silence, after which the Master of Ceremonies dismissed us in these words: "By the Power in me vested I declare the Temple closed."

So ended a really beautiful ceremony—beautifully conceived and beautifully carried out. If there is any higher form of artistic expression than great verse and great music, I have yet to learn it. I do not pretend to understand the ritual that runs like a thread of magic through these meetings of the A.˙.A.˙. I do not even know what the A.˙.A.˙. is. But I do know that the whole ceremony was impressive, artistic, and produced in those present such a feeling as Crowley must have had when he wrote:

> So shalt thou conquer Space, and lastly climb
>   The walls of Time;
> And by the golden path the great have trod
>   Reach up to God!
>
> (R. R.)

Encouraged by this preliminary success, Crowley proceeded to construct a series of seven rituals for invoking the following "planetary forces,"

I.	Saturn
II.	Jupiter
III.	Mars
IV.	Sol
V.	Venus
VI.	Mercury
VII.	Luna

The rituals were subsequently published in EQUINOX No. 6. As read, they present an extremely vivid poetic effect, organised as they are into the unity of a cosmic drama in seven acts, which begins when Man, unable to solve the riddle of existence, takes counsel of Saturn, extreme old age, and only receives after much trouble the despairing replay that there is no God. Jupiter, Mars, the Sun, Venus and Mercury are in turn invoked, but all are found wanting, because of their natures. At last the Virgin Moon appears, Madonna-like, throned and crowned, veiled and silent. She is Isis and Mary, Istar and Bhavani, Artemis and Diana, but she is still barren of hope till the great God Pan, the principle of fecundity, tears asunder the veil and reveals the hope of humanity in the Crowned and Conquering Child of the Future.

Thus briefly described, it will be realised that the Rituals as such are dignified in conception in a stupendous way, though on examination they bear marks of having been somewhat hastily composed, particularly the latter ones.

Nevertheless, Crowley, forgetting perhaps his earlier contempt for the "empty-headed Athenians," decided to perform them publicly; and proceeded indeed to give a series of public performances of the Rites in Caxton Hall. Tickets, limited to 100 in number, were issued at a price of £5 5s for admission to the seven performances.

As it happened, and it does not require much imagination to understand how it happened, he was due to provide the biggest public sensation of that autumn "season" in London. Invitations, of course, were issued to the Press (and to the Police). In the result, long news stories were published with photographs in most of the newspapers, describing the Rites with no more than the usual descriptive virtuosity of journalistic roundsmen and news editors who are accustomed not to be surprised at any occurrence provided it has a "story value"; as this undoubtedly had.

THE LOOKING GLASS

A discreditable individual, however, who is proved by his journalistic manner, exemplified hereunder, to have been either insincere and consequently a black-mailer or an unscrupulous circulation-getter; or since and consequently a prurient vice-sniffer and dolt, wormed his way into the ceremonies and abused his journalistic prerogative by publishing the following scurrilous report of the proceedings in his evanescent weekly *The Looking Glass*:

The Looking Glass.   *October 29, 1910.*

AN AMAZING SECT

The meeting or seance which we are about to describe, and to which after great trouble and considerable expense we gained admittance under an assumed name, was held in a private room at Caxton Hall.... After a great deal of manoeuvring, we managed to secure a card of admission, signed by the great Crowley himself.... When all the elect had been admitted the doors were shut, and the light, which had always been exceedingly dim, was completely extinguished, except for a slight flicker on the "altar." Then after a while more ghostly figures appeared on the stage, and a person in a red hood, supported on each side by a blue-chinned gentleman in a sort of turkish bath costume, commenced to read some gibberish, to which the attendants made responses at intervals.

More turkish bath attendants then appeared and executed a kind of Morris dance round the stage. Then the gentlemen in the red cloak made fervent appeals to the Mother of Heaven, and after a little while a not unprepossessing lady appeared, informed them that she was the Mother of Heaven, and asked if she could do anything for them. They beg her to summon the Master.... The Mother of Heaven thereupon takes up her violin and plays not unskillfully for about ten minutes, during which time the room is again plunged into complete darkness. The playing is succeeded by a loud hammering, in which all the robed figures on the stage join, and after a din sufficient to wake the Seven Sleepers the lights are turned up a little and a figure appears from a recess and asks what they want. They beseech him to let them know if there is a God, as, if not, they will amuse themselves without any fear of the consequences. The Master promises to give the matter his best attention, and, after producing a flame from the floor by the simple expedient of lifting a trap door, he retires with the Mother of Heaven "for meditation," during which time darkness again intervened. After a considerable interval he returns, flings aside a curtain on the stage, and declares that the space behind it is empty, and that there is no God. He then exhorts his followers to do as they like and make the most of this life. This is his doctrine paraphrased. Following this there is another period of darkness, during which the Master recites—very effectively be it admitted—Swinburne's

"Garden of Proserpine." After this there is more meditation, followed by an imitation dervish dance by one of the company. There is also at intervals a species of Bacchic revel by the entire company on the stage, in which an apparently very young girl takes part.

We leave it to our readers...to say whether this is not a blasphemous sect whose proceedings conceivably lend themselves to immorality of the most revolting character. Remember the doctrine which we have endeavoured faintly to outline—remember the long periods of complete darkness—remember the dances and the heavy scented atmosphere, the avowed object of which is to produce what Crowley terms an "ecstasy"—and then say if it is fitting and right that young girls and married women should be allowed to attend such performances under the guise of a new religion.

New religion indeed! It is as old as the hills. The doctrines of unbridled lust and license based on the assumption that there is no God and no hereafter have been preached from time immemorial, sometimes by hedonists and fanatics pure and simple, sometimes by charlatans whose one thought is to fill their money bags by encouraging others to gratify their depraved tastes.

In the near future we shall have more to say about this man Crowley—his history and antecedents—and those of several members of the sect.

A parenthetical testimony to the character of Mr. de Wend Fenton, editor of *The Looking Glass*, a clue to the sincerity of his virtuous indignation, a news item from the *Daily Mail* of 1913, might well be inserted here:

Mr. De Wend Fenton, Editor of the Sporting Times, was fined £10 and £5 5*s* costs at Mansion House by Alderman Sir John Knill on each of six summonses— £91 10*s* in all—for sending through the post indecent articles contained in the paper.

Such was the first of the Puritan hounds who bayed in the Groves of Eleusis, upon the scent of Aleister Crowley!

The following week, November 5th, Horatio Bottomley gave a full-page echo of De Wend Fenton's bellowing. The hunt was up! The tally-ho was sounded by John Bull's spouse, a "woman-interest" Bottomley venture now defunct, entitled *John and Mary*:

> Speaking of John reminds me to warn all my women and girl readers against a dangerous "new religion," somewhat on the Abode of Love lines—only, if anything, more repulsive—which is being exploited by the so-called poet, Aleister Crowley. You will read all about it in Thursday's *John Bull*—a lady member of its staff having, I understand, managed to obtain admission to one of Crowley's *seances*—fortunately escaping with nothing worse than a kiss in the dark!

The bellowing of *John Bull* was as follows:

John Bull.   *November 5, 1910.*

IS A NEW SMYTH-PIGOTT AMONG US?
Mr. Aleister Crowley's Blasphemous and
Prurient Propaganda.

A "new religion" is usually viewed with suspicion in this country, but Mr. Crowley is just the person for such an enterprise. He is a man of good birth and education, with distinguished, almost pontifical, manners. He has travelled over all the unusual parts of the world and investigated fantastic things with zeal, if not with discretion. He has probed the secret recesses of most Oriental religions and has made a special study of all the endless literature of magic and mysticism. Though he has never yet succeeded in catching the long ear of the public, he has been a voluminous writer, and has published works which fill many shelves. "Knox Om Pax" and "777" have already been noticed in this journal. To the uninitiated, they appear like the outpourings of an extremely clever lunatic, now solemnly revealing the secrets of the ancients, now running off into the most delightly nonsense, now assuming the role of the preacher, now frankly pulling legs. His chief efforts have been concentrated upon the composition of really remarkable poetry. His rhythm and metre and melody are often quite perfect, and as a lord of language he runs Swinburne very close. Often he goes very near to the borderland of insanity.

His work, however, is spoiled by the intrusion of wild, erotic, and disgusting images and startling blasphemies, which restrict his writing to private circulation, though it possesses an artistic enchantment quite apart from its appeal to pruriency and debauchery.

His present "mission" was heralded in March of last year by a portly publication called the "Equinox." The idea, evidently, is to attract the public to the teachings of mediæval alchemists or magicians. The propaganda consists in assembling a number of ladies and gentlemen in a dark room, where poems are recited in sonorous tones and a violin is played with considerable expressions, amid choking clouds of incense, varied by barbaric dances, sensational interludes of melodrama, blasphemy and erotic suggestion.

* * * * *

Our Representative's Report.

By special favour, or good fortune, or both, I was able to get free admission into the chamber of mysteries, which others less fortunate than I could not enter without paying in advance a fee of £5.... The room was in semi-darkness.... A large cushion was given me to sit on. "The Master of the Temple" was at last aroused.

Our Representative Embraced.

He came forward, crouched behind the cauldron, and recited a most blood-curdling composition, filled with horrible allusions to "the stony state of dead men's eyes," etc., etc. After all, one couldn't blame him for getting angry at being disturbed, I suppose. However, suddenly he lifted what looked like a tin of Nestle's milk, and pouring the contents on the flame, extinguished the fire, declared that "there is no God," that everybody was free to do just as he or she liked, and left the audience in utter darkness! Not the slightest ray of light entered the room, and the atmosphere seemed heavier and more oppressive than ever. There was a sound as of people moving quietly about, which added to the uncanniness. How long this lasted I do not know, but all of a sudden an arm was placed round my neck, and a moustache pressed to my check—someone had kissed me!

* * * * *

Mystical figures were moving before me, and I watched, fascinated.... What a weird picture it was!... There was more violin music, and a wild barbaric dance in the misty, smoky blue light.... I had had enough, and was heartily glad when it was all over.

JONES *vs*. LOOKING GLASS

Naturally, Crowley took no notice of this sort of thing. Already stated, respectable journalism had dealt fairly enough by him. The *Bystander* actually commissioned him to write a series of articles in exposition of his ideas. Crowley agreed and his reasoned exposition was published. Meanwhile the *Looking Glass* continued to publish attacks upon him, assiduously digging up any facts in his life which might be given an unpleasant interpretation, and duly giving them that interpretation. Crowley, like many another man, had been divorced. De Wend Fenton played on this theme to its utmost, digging up the law reports for material. The worst he could find, however, was that Crowley had committed adultery, not at all an unusual sin, in England, particularly among respondents in divorce cases!

The story must now return to the Brethren of the Golden Dawn, gnashing their teeth impotently over the publication of their rituals in the EQUINOX and the checkmate of McGregor Mathers in the Court of Appeals.

De Wend Fenton's attack developed an entirely new virility and venom:

> Further information has reached us from an unimpeachable source as to the past record of this man, who dares to put himself forward as a high priest....

It is evident from what follows that the "unimpeachable source" lay concealed among the "Rosicrucians" whose own doctrines were so respectfully mirrored in the *Looking Glass*.

In 1898 Crowley became of member of the Rosicrucian Order, a very ancient association, whose principal object is the study of the mystic philosophy of ancient religions, and which professes a vast amount of traditional lore on this and kindred subjects, while requiring from its members due respect and honour for religious ideas, as well as good moral character.

There followed the passages upon which George Cecil Jones subsequently based his action against De Wend Fenton for libel.

Two of Crowley's friends and introducers are still associated with him; one, the rascally sham Buddhist monk Allan Bennett; the other a person of the name of George Cecil Jones, who was for some time employed at Basingstoke in metallurgy, but of late has had some sort of small merchant's business in the City. Crowley and Bennett lived together, and there were rumours of unmentionable immoralities which were carried on under their roof....

The remainder of the article was taken up with scurrilous allegations, of which the following are characteristic:

Soon after this Crowley began to shield himself under different aliases.... His aliases would grace an Old Bailey criminal.... In 1900 he began to show up in his true colours. Being sent from Paris to London on certain matters connected with the Order, he enormously exceeded his instructions, and stole certain property of the Order, which he took up with him to Boleskine. His next exploit was to steal the jewels of a lady, the wife of an English officer, as well as to extort money by threats. She obtained a warrant for his arrest, but he fled the country, having in the meantime, obtained a considerable amount from a well-known signer. It only remains for us to add that he was formally expelled from the Rosicrucian Order as a man of evil character and acts....

And, as a peroration, all the category of unmentionable vice was alleged in that veiled language of innuendo which only a coward knows how to use:

Many of his poems are of the most obscene and revolting character. Other statements about him we refrain from printing, as they are of too horrible a nature, but we think we have said enough to show that our previous attacks on him and his orgies were more than justified....

Crowley himself took no notice whatever of De Wend Fenton or Horatio Bottomley. He was not spiritually vulnerable to such venom and thought that the obvious absurdity of such propaganda would defeat its own ends without any active assistance from him. He went on with the task of preparing the vernal EQUINOX. George Cecil Jones, however, issued a writ, and in due course the "Rosicrucians" again had an opportunity to amuse the Courts of Justice and the readers of newspapers.

A TRIAL FROM "ALICE IN WONDERLAND"

The libel action, Jones *vs. The Looking Glass*, would almost undoubtedly take first place among the comic trials of English history. At one point the Judge remarked:

> This trial is getting very much like the trial in "Alice in Wonderland." (Laughter.)

The evidence of both parties was continuously punctuated by laughter in Court. Crowley himself was in Court throughout, enjoying the jokes to the full, though neither side called him to give evidence—an astonishing fact considering that, if anything, his habits and characteristics were mainly in dispute:

> The action was brought by Mr. George Cecil Jones, a consulting chemist, against the publishers, editor and printers of the paper known as The Looking Glass, in respect of certain statements connecting him with one Crowley, who was alleged to be a person of disgraceful and criminal character, who was alleged to be the founder of a sect styled "THE EQUINOX." (*Times Law Reports*.)

Portions of the evidence are transcribed below. From the very beginning the atmosphere of a Gilbert and Sullivan opera was indicated:

> *(Evidence of George Cecil Jones.)*
>
> Counsel: Were you never a member of the Rosicrucian Order?
> Witness: No.
> Counsel: Have you never applied to become a member of the Rosicrucian Order?

Witness: No; honestly I do not know except from having read the 17th century tract whether there is or was such a Society as the Rosicrucian Order.
Council: Have you ever heard of Volo Noscere?
Witness: Yes, quite well.
Mr. Justice Scrutton: You both seem to know what you are talking about, but I do not. (*idem*)

(Evidence relating to the previous action, Mathers vs. Crowley.)

Counsel: Was the action brought against Mr. Crowley to restrain him from publishing the ritual of the Order in violation of his obligation?
Witness: I never saw the statement of claim. I do not know what the action was brought about.
Counsel: Was the complaint made against Mr. Crowley that he was publishing the ritual of the Order?
Witness: No
Mr. Justice Scrutton: Was it instructions as to the Devil, or what?
Witness: Very nearly.
Counsel: I am not a member of the order.

(Dealing with Crowley's character)

Counsel: Crowley has not brought any action?
Witness: I believe not.
Counsel: Is Crowley here in Court?
Witness: Yes, I can see him.

Counsel: Do not you say that Crowley is a gentleman of unblemished character?
Witness: I have no reason to suppose that his character is a bit worse than yours.
Counsel: He is a man you would not hesitate to introduce to your wife?
Witness: My wife knows him very well.
Counsel: You are still to the present day associated with Crowley?
Witness: He is still a friend of mine.
Counsel: And an intimate friend of yours?
Witness: Yes; no particular significance attaches to the word. I see him once in two months; we talk on the telephone once a week, we are very friendly when we meet; he comes to me with any difficulties that he has.

(Cross-examined by Mr. De Wend Fenton.)

Q: You said that there was very little that was accurate in our article?
A: I should describe that page on which my name is mentioned as the finest collection of lies you could crowd on to one page.
Q: Do you not think it rather strange that Crowley has never taken action against us?
A: I do think it very strange.
Q: I think you said that if Crowley was in the box he would probably admit he was not sane?
A: I think he probably would but I do not think for a moment that you would get him certified.

(Evidence of Samuel Sydney Liddell Macgregor.)
(Daily Telegraph Report.)

Called by the name of "Macgregor," the witness, after taking the oath, asked whether his full name was desired. It having been intimated that it was desired, witness announced a long list of Christine names, and the surname of "Mathers." "Mathers," he explained amidst laughter, "dates from 1603 when the name of Macgregor was suppressed."

Counsel: You commonly go under the name Macgregor? –Yes, from my great-great grandfather, from whom I have a Franco-Scottish title.

Are you known as Count Macgregor de Glenstae? —Yes.

Does the Rosicrucian Order go back to considerable antiquity? —Yes.

Did it fall into abeyance and did you revive it? –Yes, with two others.

Witness added that the plaintiff introduced Crowley into the Rosicrucian Order. Crowley was subsequently expelled. He had known Crowley to go under several different names. "Once," said witness, "he called himself Macgregor, and with hardly any knowledge of the history of the name. (Laughter.) He couldn't even tell me what line of Macgregor he came from." (Much laughter.)

(Mathers cross-examined.)

Counsel: Is it not a fact that your name is Samuel Liddell Mathers? —Yes, or Macgregor Mathers.

Your original name was Samuel Liddell Mathers? —Undoubtedly.

Did you subsequently assume the name of Macgregor? — The name of Macgregor dates from 1603.

Your name was Macgregor in 1603? (Much laughter.) —Yes; if you like to put it that way.

You have called yourself Count Macgregor of Glensae? —Oh yes.

You have also called yourself the Chevalier Macgregor? —No. You are confusing me with some of Crowley's aliases.

Have you ever suggested to anybody that you had any connection with King James IV of Scotland? — Every Scotchman who dates from an ancient family must have had some connection with King James IV.

Have you ever stated that King James IV of Scotland never died? —Yes; that is a matter of common tradition among all occult bodies.

Do you assert that James IV of Scotland is in existence today? —I refuse to answer your question.

And that his existence to-day is embodied in yourself? –Certainly not. You are confusing me with Crowley's aliases. (Laughter.)

You believe in the traditions? —That is my private business.

His Lordship (to counsel): The "Flying Dutchman" is another if you want to pursue the subject. (Laughter.)

Witness: And, again, "The Wandering Jew." (Laughter.)

Council: Have you any occupation? –That is as you like to take it. For a man of no occupation I am probably the most industrious man living. (Laughter.)

(His Lordship's Summing up.)

His Lordship said that as regards some of the accusations made against Crowley no evidence had been offered, but it had been shown that he wrote, published, and advertised literature of a most disgusting character. The jury must carefully consider how far what had been said identified the plaintiff with Crowley's character and conduct. He should leave them three questions:

1. Were the words and statements complained of defamatory of the plaintiff?
2. If yes, were the statements of facts substantially true?
3. If yes, were the comments founded on those statements of facts fair?

The jury answered all three questions in the affirmative, and on those findings judgment was entered for the defendants.

It will be noticed in connection with this weird action that the statements in the Looking Glass referring to George Cecil Jones were found to be defamatory, and substantially true—but that the publication caused no damage to the plaintiff! This was certainly a fitting conclusion to the "Alice in Wonderland" trial. The fact that Crowley was not called upon to give evidence for either side, though he was manifestly the villain of the melodrama, is sufficiently interesting as indicating the uneasiness which his personality could inspire, both in friends and foes. One of Crowley's books, with passages underlined in pencil, was passed up to the Judge and jury despite protests by counsel against its admissibility as evidence. The Judge himself frequently expressed a doubt as to the admissibility of any evidence against Crowley, in view of the fact that Crowley was not a party to this case. There was a long legal argument on this point, the Judge finally ruling in favour of some evidence against Crowley with the remarks, "this is a very odd case, but I think it is admissible.... I cannot say that no statement made by Crowley is inadmissible." Doubtless his Lordship's *bon mot* about the "Alice in Wonderland" trial was the brightest possible description of the whole episode.

Again Crowley found himself featuring as the "hero" of important news stories in the whole popular Press of the land. There can be no doubt that it was this episode which first gave general currency to the "legend" proper. It certainly laid a solid and deep foundation for the edifice of slander which was later to be erected in his name.

THE EQUINOX CONTINUES

Nos. 5 and 6 appeared, despite the distracting incidents just related. Crowley was apparently quite unaffected by the proceedings which would have given a lesser man more than sufficient preoccupation. Two characteristic Press commentaries are appended:

Equinox No. 5.

Far and away the best number that has hitherto appeared. A ballet by Aleister Crowley contains many passages of extreme beauty and leonine vigor.... A remarkable article by Ananda Matteya.... One of the most remarkable and illuminating articles on the Qabalah.... A magnificent essay upon number. It is impossible to praise this work of art too highly.... The amount of knowledge and benefit to be obtained by the owner and diligent student is almost infinite.... This book will be as the Wine of Life to mystics, and to those who confidently expect a revaluation of values in the history of the world. (*Occult Review.*)

EQUINOX NO. 6.

Mr. Aleister Crowley among his multifarious activities, finds time to contribute the major portion of the "Equinox" (he is the editor?) and writes with equal facility in verse and prose.... His three Poems for *Jane Chéron* are of a remarkable, if somewhat decadent, beauty.... Into the "Rites of Eleusis" Mr. Crowley has woven a number of poems of great power. These alone are worth the money. ...A remarkable story by Mr. M. Nay.... This extraordinary volume.... Excellent reading. (*Daily Mail.*)

HAIL MARY!

It may be considered that Crowley really went too far in submitting anonymously, about this time, a volume of devotional verses to Burns & Oates, the Catholic publishers. The verses were hymns in praise of Mary, though the name Isis could easily have been substituted. Wilfred Meynell was quite guileless, and published the book under the title of AMPHORA. It was only when authorship of the poems was being attributed to a famous actress of the time (!) that Crowley revealed his complicity, and had the volume re-issued under his own name, with the title Hail Mary! (1912).

The Catholic Press took the joke fairly well, all things considered:

> Here truly is a plenteous and varied feast for the lovers of tuneful verse! As far as we can gather from his other works, the author is not a Catholic, perhaps not even, strictly speaking, a Christian; but here we have page after page of most exquisite praise of Her... until one marvels at the poet's fecundity of concept, imagery, and fit expression. (*Catholic Times*.)
>
> Not without a certain lyrical sweetness. Devotion to the Mother of God is the subject of all the poems, and it seems odd coming from one who is understood to be a worshipper at strange, exotic, and forbidden shrines. But the artistic temperament is doubtlessly accountable.... (*Catholic Herald*.)

Lascelles Abercrombie, writing in the *Daily News*, seems to have been rather pained by the apparent *volte face*:

> Mr. Aleister Crowley is a very interesting poet, not so much for any great originality in his technique, as for the passionate tenacity with which he holds to a mystical creed, put forth in an elaborate and eclectic symbolism. ...He has not managed to hymn Mary in anything like the strain of poetry which the worship of Hecate once drew from him. Does this mean that, after all, Hecate means more to him than Mary?

And in the *English Review* appeared a commentary, delightful to read after the sordidness of the *Looking Glass* affair; delightful even to this day for its clean statement of the real problem of Aleister Crowley—a challenge to 1930 as much as it was a challenge in 1912:

> We crave for poetry in England, but we do not like poets unless they are exceedingly conventional, when we can laureate them, because in the national search for what is called character we condemn vagaries which are the attributes of genius. Every school girl reads Shelley, yet how badly we treated him! Byron is not allowed to rest in Poet's Corner. We have treated Swinburne as if he were Crippen. And we have treated Mr. Aleister Crowley in much the same way. Yet Aleister Crowley is one of our few real poets. He has written things in ambergris which will never die. Some years ago a little book of verse appeared, called AMPHORA, which being anonymous was attributed to an actress. It bore a strong religious note, an ecstatic sense, and it was at once recognized as genuine poetry. Now it has come forth again, retitled HAIL MARY, and signed Aleister Crowley. We hope it will be widely read, and serve as an introduction to some of Mr. Crowley's other works of poetry. Particularly we hope the Church will look at it. They will find a religious sense that will astonish some of them. The real trouble about Mr. Crowley is this: he is a true poet—he cannot compromise. The persecution of silly and unkind men has wounded him. It is for literary men now to come forward and stand by him.

Literary men to come forward and stand by him! Will any eminent literary man of to-day join the undistinguished compiler of the present book in asking that Aleister

Crowley should even now be judged as a poet, for his poetry? Is there any (unmystical) Brotherhood of the Pen? Historians of the future may take an interest in the answer to this question. I think that I am establishing in this compilation of his Press-cuttings that Aleister Crowley has many claims to be regarded as a distinguished poet. He may also be a distinguished wag, or scallaway, or harum-scarum, or whatnot, but he is a distinguished poet, and the poet has the right to be heard, for his poetry.

TWO MORE BOOKS OF POETRY.

Besides Hail Mary! (and not to mention the EQUINOX, Nos. 7 and 8) two more books of poetry by Aleister Crowley were issued in 1912. These were MORTADELLO and SIR PALAMEDES THE SARACEN. It is interesting to record the opinions of two "men of letters" of this period, Harold Monro and Gilbert Cannan, who had apparently decided to give Crowley the serious consideration his growing achievement warranted.

Writing of MORTADELLO in the Poetry Review, Gilbert Cannan found a stumbling-block:

> Mr. Crowley is an amazing creature. He refuses to be taken seriously. His bloodthirsty, lecherous play he calls a comedy. It is a riotous farce. Intoxication—of blood, of words, of hysteria, of lust—takes the place of imagination. The play is exciting, but most amusing in its invective.... Mr. Crowley has talent, scores of talents, but, seemingly, no power to use, discipline, or develop them. It would be splendid to take him seriously, but then—one cannot. He has abundant humour—a most necessary ingredient in a poet's composition—but that, too, is untamed.

In the *Poetry Review*, also, Harold Monro reviewed SIR PALAMEDES, and confessed himself unable to find a niche for its author: an honest, if quite evasive, solution of the "serious" critic's problem:

> Seriously speaking it is a religious poem, and a great work of art. Superficially speaking, it is the master limerick of a buffoon; again, seriously speaking, it is the epic of the eternal Seeker.... Mr. Crowley is extraordinarily entertaining, and of course he is also much more than entertaining. SIR PALAMEDES, though probably not his best work, should on no account be missed. It is a work that superficial criticism might as easily compare to some of the productions of Byron, as overlook with a sneer. I doubt, in fact, whether the question of its place in literature is one to be decided by contemporary criticism at all. I, at any rate, will not commit myself to attempting to decision.

END OF THE EQUINOX

In 1913 Crowley paid a visit to Moscow, not to see Lenin and Trotsky, or Gog or Magog of the Apocalypse in order to bring about the millennium as might be supposed by the credulous, but merely in order to enjoy himself, by visiting a place somewhat unlike London. Nevertheless, he managed to publish the last two volumes of the EQUINOX, thereby completing ten volumes — or, more precisely, the ten Parts of Volume One. He indicated that the next Volume would consist of "Ten Numbers of Silence," to balance all that speech: a commendable enough decision which the actual coming of Armageddon, or something very like it, in the Great War, made easily possible of achievement.

He also published, and I do not pretend to understand where he found the time and energy to do it, two Books on Technical Magick, during this year—the BOOK OF LIES, and BOOK FOUR.

THE BOOK OF LIES

Every page of this book is lined with a heavy black border. The first page of "text" is an Interrogation mark ("The Hunchback"). The second page is an Exclamation Mark ("The Soldier"). The full title of the work is:

THE BOOK OF LIES
which is also falsely called
BREAKS.
The Wanderings or Falsifications of the One Thought
of
FRATER PERDURABO.
Which Thought is Itself Untrue.

It is puzzling enough work to the layman, for whom, however, I presume, it was not intended primarily. H. S. Redgrove expressed the following opinions of it in the *Occult Review*:

> I am not at all sure what is the meaning (assuming there to be one) of this fantastic book by Mr. Aleister Crowley. Some of its chapters seem entire nonsense, but in others I can discern something of a philosophy which is a negation of philosophy; which regards thought as the excrement of mind, and reason as foolishness.... Certainly such philosophy as this is a lie, if that is the meaning of the title.
>
> But indeed, I am inclined to regard the book rather as a fantastic and elaborate joke; and I can imagine its author laughing at the thought of its readers striving to extract a profound meaning out of words which have

no meaning. Certainly, there are times when Mr. Crowley is very funny.... It is hard to resist laughing.... But I do not think Mr. Crowley's humour is always in the best taste, nor can I always see the point of his jokes, and at times his words and suggestions seem quite deliberately and unnecessarily blasphemous and objectionable. I regard sexual symbolism as a valid method of expression; but I like it unperverted.

BOOK FOUR

This was, in its first part, a brilliant exposition of Yoga, resulting from Crowley's own researches and experiences in the East. The *African Times* found a description which will bear repeating here:

> This exotic exudation of esoteric exegesis...

a phrase which we may perhaps accept, with all its implications, as summarising, indeed, a great deal of the writing of the whole Equinox period, however much we may admire the clear poetry, the dazzling humour, and the amazing versatility of that period, considered in it purely literary aspects.

A CAMBRIDGE POET

At the end of 1913 an anthology was published entitled CAMBRIDGE POETS, 1900-13. Crowley was included in the Anthology, being given indeed quite a considerable space. This looks, on the surface, like recognition. Unfortunately, however, the editors, sharing perhaps the common failings of anthologists, for it would not be charitable to attribute malice to them, had made a collection almost of Crowley's worst poetry, his least personally distinctive verse. The *Manchester Guardian* violently commented:

Far the worst lack of discretion of compilation is the devotion of 20 pages to Mr. Aleister Crowley, whose overblown rhetoric is so well-known that it surely might have been omitted altogether.

More soothing is the naïveté of the *Birmingham Post*:

> From Mr. Aleister Crowley's strange and mystical books the editor has selected some 20 pages of poetry which we have contemplated with considerable astonishment, but little admiration, although we recognise a Promethean grandeur which elsewhere we seek vainly.

NINETEEN FOURTEEN

That "Promethean Grandeur" had been Crowley's cardinal sin against his Age. We "seek it vainly elsewhere," not only in the pages of the Cambridge anthology, but amongst all the joblot of poets of that collapsed Edwardian age. The other poets, without exception, were shirking their responsibilities as Makers. Alone, amongst a crowd of obsessed with minutæ, Aleister Crowley was attempting, and it does not even matter if he failed, to formulate a poetic consciousness of the human Universal. Poetry was petering out into triviality, indeed the whole Nation was petering out spiritually; and Crowley had the courage to tackle his poet's job of re-integration. He will yet be honoured for this courage, even if his achievement be condemned. He belonged to no schools or coteries; he was romantic and wild and boisterous when all others were becoming so "refined" that they almost vanished in transparency. No one could suggest seriously that poets like Dowson, and Middleton, and Yeats, will ever be placed in the great succession of English poets who worked cosmically—the major poets who worked widely on the whole human canvas! Shakespeare, and Blake, and Milton, and Shelley, and Swinburne with all their faults; even Browning. After Swinburne and Browning, is there one poet, to our day, who has worked on that Grand Plan of poetry which shirks nothing human?

In *scope*, in cosmic self-definition, in the Grand Manner unashamed—only Aleister Crowley!

For all his perverseness, for all his rocketing violence, for all his downright folly, he is full of meat and blood where his contemporaries are most stuffed with straw—in the vitals.

I leave the discussion at present with this dogmatic statement, dogmatic because I cannot prove it, and cannot expect readers to believe it, until the day, which may never come in our lifetime, when his COMPLETE WORKS are available to students possessed of some time-perspective of this Age. At present there is no man living who possesses a complete collection of the Works of Aleister Crowley. Not even Crowley himself! Some editors of the future will have a fine job—collecting those dozens and dozens of exquisitely printed small editions in order to establish definitive texts!

Separately, each one of those books in turn has astonished reviewers, sophisticated or simpletons, as I have shown in the quotation. I think nobody has had the chance to see his work as a whole. I do not pretend to have made more than a preliminary survey myself, for the purposes of this study. But that glimpse has been enough to establish my present contention—that he has worked grandly as a poet, has tackled the poetic synthesis heroically, while all his contemporaries funked that synthesis. With this, I leave opinion, and return to my job of collecting documentary facts.

THE WAR

CHAPTER IV

The War
1914-1919

Long before the War, Crowley gave plenty of evidence in his poetry of his contempt for pre-War England, that was for the England of the victorious middle classes in their apotheosis under Queen Victoria, Mr. Gladstone—and, in a word, petty commercialism rampant. As early as 1900 he had written in CARMEN SECULARE:

> O England! England, mighty England falls!
> None shall lament her lamentable end!
> The Voice of Justice thunders at her walls.
> She would not hear. She shall not comprehend!
> The nations keep their mocking carnivals;
> She hath not left a friend!

in a voice which one cannot help likening to that of an ancient Biblical prophet, wild from the desert, thundering "Woe!" before the trembling court of a potentate.

I cannot see that it is "unpatriotic" for a poet to chasten his own people—it is rather a sign of the poet's deep love. The physician does not hate his cancerous patient. Isaiah did not hate the Jews. Isaiah was a patriot. Crowley is a patriot and he loves when he denounces. Unless this be conceded as possible, there can be no forgiveness for Crowley—at any rate so long as the War's rancours last.

As a satirist, he was certainly strong meat. The following verses, from THE WORLD'S TRAGEDY (1911) are characteristic:

> And if I write for England, who will read?
> As if, when moons of Ramazan recede,
> Some fatuous angel-porter should deposit
> His perfect wine within the privy closet!
> "What do they know, who only England know?"
> Only what England paints its face to show.

> Love mummied and relabelled "chaste affection,"
> And lust excused as "natural selection,"
> Caligula upbraids the cruel cabby,
> And Nero birches choir-boys in the Abbey;
> Semiramis sandpapered to a simper,
> And Clytemnæstra whittled to a whimper!
> The austerities of Loyola? to seek!
> But—let us have a "self-denial week"!
> The raptures of Teresa are hysteric'
> But—let us giggle at some fulsome cleric!
> "The age refines! You lag behind," God knows!
> Plus ça change, plus c'est la même chose.

> To call forced labour slavery is rude,
> "Terminologic inexactitude."
> This from the masters of the winds and waves
> Whose cotton-mills are crammed with British slaves!
> Men pass their nights with German-Jewish whores,
> Their days in keeping "aliens" from our shores.
> They turn their eyes up at a Gautier's tale,
> And run a maisonette in Maida Vale.

Your titles—oh! how proud you are to wear them?
—What about "homo quatuor literarum?
The puissant all their time to vice devote;
The impotent (contented) pay to gloat.
The strumpet's car wheels splash the starving maiden
In Piccadilly, deadlier than Aden.
"England expects a man to do his duty."
He calls truth lies, and sneers at youth and beauty.
Pay cash for love and fancies he has won it—
Duty means church, where he thanks God he's done it!

Later (August 28th, 1914) he wrote an article entitled THE VINDICATION OF NIETZSCHE, the tone of which may be gauged from the following excerpts:

> Entrenched in the morass of bibliolatry, crouching in the bastions of Fort Grundy, the old Guard of Victorianism died and did not surrender.... We have had a credit system which when analyzed meant that we were all pretending to be rich, a social system in which we all pretended to be squires at the least. We had Dukes who never led, Marquesses with no marches to ward, Knights who could barely sit a donkey; we called our slattern slaveys lady helps, our prostitutes soiled doves, our grumbling mumbling politicians statesmen.
>
> We had Progressed. Lady Pyjama Noisette had a headache to the tune of a paragraph—10 lines. Sandsugar v. Sandsugar and Pintpot—a column. A piddling little quack doctor poisons his bitch of a wife and runs off with his fool of a typist—the business of the world is suspended until he is cinematographically hanged.

A prominent writer calls attention to himself by the device of calling attention to the pangs of the slaughtered oxen; another affirms his brotherhood with the Chicago Pig. Countless thousands turn Vegetarian, and then quarrel as to whether it is or is not True Vegetarianism to eat eggs. The war between the Fruitarians and the Nut-faddists neatly came to a cross word! I knew a "man" who refused to eat bread because it was a fermented drink! A friend of mind knew an Anarchist who refused cocoa because it excited his animal passions!

It was in this mood, therefore, that Crowley confronted the War, welcomed the War, undoubtedly. For an account of his movements and motives during the War period, during practically the whole of which he was in America, I must refer those interested to that portion of his Autobiography, now in the press, which deals with this period, under the title of THE LAST STRAW. I here reprint without further comment at *précis* of that statement, prepared for the Press by Crowley's secretary at the time when he was "in trouble" (1929) with the French authorities:

THE LAST STRAW
(precis)

The essence of my adventures during the late War may be put in a nutshell. At the outbreak of the War I was in Switzerland engaged in solitary climbs among the Alps. On my return to England I was foiled in my attempts to fight for my country, as I had been interrupted in my efforts to climb the Alps by an attack of phlebitis which kept me in bed for some six weeks, from the middle of September to the end of October, 1914.

I was warned that the slightest movement might result in sudden death, and advised, that even upon recovery, I would never be able, in all probability, to climb a mountain again. I had the strange idea—how strange to England in 1914!—that war was a very serious matter, and that it was "my country, right or wrong." I thought I had ideas and virility, and that my country therefore needed me. This event indicated my fatuity. At that time any man in England who suggested the advisability of conscription was the worst kind of traitor. Conscription was the very thing we were fighting against. From my sick bed, I dictated an article called "Thorough" in which I said: "Commandeer every man and every munition in the country. This is not a continental quarrel—this is life and death for England. We don't want debates in Parliament or in Colony Hatch. We want a dictator." No editor would publish it.

When I left Switzerland on the outbreak of the War, I went to Paris, and was amazed at the *sang froid* of the people. Going on to England, to offer my services to the authorities, I was disgusted at the sharp contrast between the calm courage of the French and the hysterical fear, culminating in the campaign of hate, of my own people. The German was now a monster like a bogy in a nightmare, and it was useless to struggle against him. At the same time he was a coward, without discipline, courage, and morale—with a talent only for rape, torture, and theft—a brute who did not dare to advance unless behind a screen of Belgian nuns. I was then more convinced that I was needed by my country, by England. In my excitement, I had the hallucination that England needed men. I went here and there, trying to find a place to help. "What about me? I have some little reputation as a man of letters—a critic. It is true my phlebitis affected my left leg, but I am expert in cipher—I read and write French as well as I write English, and the world knows how well that is. I have a fair acquaintance with a dozen other languages, including Hindustani. My leg will keep me out of the war as effectively as Wilson will keep America—is there nothing I can do to serve my country?" But from August to the end of October, 1914, I had tried every means to get the Government to use me—without success.

* * * * *

I accepted an invitation to go to America, and there chance showed me a way for which I was peculiarly fitted; a part by which I might conceivably play as important a part in the War as any man living. The price of this success was moral courage to the limit. I must beggar myself for funds, friends, and honour for the time being.

While waiting in America for certain of my manuscripts and books to arrive, I occupied myself in observing the attitude of New Yorkers to the War. It needed but a brief inquiry to see that Americans meant to make money out of the War by exporting food and munition to the Allies. (How could they make money out of Germany while the British Navy maintained an effective blockade against the Central Powers?)

It was quite a little while before it dawned upon me that we were going to have to depend upon America for these necessities: that our industrialism has so sapped the economy of our resources that civilization was going to seek salvation at the hands of the barbarian. It is the old old story being continually retold. This was the fatal error, pregnant with the catastrophe which was death to Greece and a creeping paralysis to Rome. The same delusion will gangrene England within the lifetime of most men of military age unless she will realize that gold is dross; that her poets, her artists, and her scholars are her very soul.

If one had asked the New Yorker: "What are you going to do about it? What of ravished Belgium? What of violated treaties?" The answer would casually have come: "Don't be foolish! Safety first is the rule here! If you want to fight, go to Europe. If you want to talk war, go to hell; this country is neutral." This was the business sort, the calculating cold-blooded person. Is not the dollar God, and does not God fight for the general who has the preponderance of artillery?

But amidst the bewilderment and conflict which reigned all the while, there were a few generous people, those who were educated. They were rare; but they were on our side.

* * * * *

I did not care whether my country was right or wrong. I could see both sides. So finding myself temporarily held up in New York, I bethought myself whether I could not by some means serve England.

Through certain accidents, needless to narrate here, I met George Sylvester Viereck, a man of considerable talent. He knew the world well, being undeceived by the humbug of public men and the prostitute antics of the Press; his point of view possessed the sanity which came from the second-rater's perception of the necessity of compromise. He was a man of suave insinuating manners and address, a man of considerable political experience and address, a man of considerable political experience and immense intellectual capacity. But his intelligence was not sufficiently subtle to comprehend this moral paradox in myself. I am English and I love England. Yet I praised Germany—I sympathized with Germany—I justified Germany, and he erroneously deduced that I was pro-German. During one of his conversations, it dawned upon me that here was the real headquarters of the German propaganda, the publishers of *The Fatherland*.

I then looked for what Americans call "The man higher up." I finally found such a candidate for the secret direction of the German propaganda in Professor Hugo Münsterberg. As it happens, he was an old enemy of mine, we having quarrelled about philosophy and physics. He was an intensely positive man, brutally matter-of-fact, but capable of appreciating subtlety, and far more open to new facts and theories than most of his opponents supposed. He knew psychology; he knew men, he understood business. His arrogance was immense, and in his capacity of instructor at Harvard University, he had acquired the habits of a leader. So much I knew, and my mind pictured a duel—thrilling and romantic.

But the facts were less enthralling. The professor had the great German gift of Being Always Right. Thus my task was much simplified, for I had merely to keep on telling him how very right he was, and under this treatment he soon ceased to gauge the temper of the community correctly, and finally became violent and stupid.

My immediate problem, though, was to confirm Viereck in my conviction that I really was pro-German. I found him very sympathetic about Irish Independence; and there being a number of families of my name, Crowley, in America, who had come direct from Ireland, I billed myself accordingly as the only and original Sinn Feiner. My trouble was that I knew but little (but this is a minor point in America) about the Irish question, but it was made easier—Viereck wanted to believe—and did, after I wrote some rancorous nonsense about Irish Independence. Having thus established myself as an Irish Rebel, I went away and considered what I should set myself to do. I soon concluded that the propaganda of *The Fatherland*, in which the German cause was presented with the utmost clarity, logic, scholarship and moderation, was infernally dangerous to the Allied Cause. I talked to my friends about it. They thought little of it at the time, and so I was left consummate my own plans, alone—in sheer solitude,—misunderstood!

I decided on a course of action. I would write for *The Fatherland*. I would work up Viereck gradually, first with relatively reasonable attacks on England to rabid extravagances which would achieve my object— that of revolting every comparatively sane human being on earth.

I proved the *Lusitania* to be a Man-of-War. I translated atrocity not merely into military necessity, but actually into moral uplift, and placed golden haloes on the statue of Von Hindenberg. And one day, that of the murder of Edith Cavell, I go drunk—drunk with rage and indignation. I sat down and wrote an article. I pictured Von Bissing as a modern Jesus Christ—a great-souled, simple-minded trusting German, with humanity and the world at heart, extending his hand, with tears in his eyes, saying "Nurse Cavell, I trust you." She reacts as Judas, and I thereupon conclude by a display of rhetoric—equalled only by the bare-faced gullibility in which it was received and swallowed—in which she is welcomed to Hell by Lucrezia Borgia and other unpopular ladies.

It made me weep for Germany to think that Viereck actually published such hideous and transparent irony without turning a hair. (America does not understand irony and satire; sarcasm is absolutely wasted on its people.) But are there tears salt enough to weep for England, when on thinks that few or none of my countrymen could read the bitterness, anger and heart-break between the lines of that comic travesty of blasphemy. Everybody assumed that the irritating most transparent balderdash I wrote for *The Fatherland* must be the stark treason which the Germans were stupid enough to think it was. But my Germans were loud in their congratulations. I advocated in the style of a real German Professor the "Unrestricted Submarine Warfare," secretly calculating (rightly so, as time showed) that so outrageous a violation of all law and human decency would be the LAST STRAW and force America to come in on our side.

But with this "success" there came a blow. A friend from a certain British consulate turned disgustingly on me after reading the articles (before I explained my self-appointed task, for the sake of England) and growled: "I didn't know you were a German." I admit I was downhearted! How could we hope to win the war if Englishmen had got so hysterical as that?

* * * * *

The situation changed. When America entered the War, the Department of Justice, having both brains and the audacity to use them, got busy. They swiftly realized, as I had done before, that the intellectual of the Viereck and Münsterberg type is infinitely more dangerous than the clumsy kind who blow up bridges in places that don't matter. The Department used me to the full, and I did my bit.

In the upshot, at last I got money enough to settle my affairs in New York, where I had been dodging starvation for five years. That legend of my growing fat on German gold! I lost no time in coming home to England. My conscience was clear. I had been loyal to England. I had suffered for her sake more than any man. I had fought the good fight, despising the shame. Starvation and solitude of soul and body! But I was content. I care nothing for public opinion; nothing for fame or success. My attitude is unaltered by time. I still think England pot as black as the German kettle, but I am still willing to die in defence of the pot!

Such is the poet's own interpretation of actions which, to say the least, risked a quite contrary interpretation. Certainly not Aleister Crowley, amongst living men, could have been so quixotic in his defence of the "pot." I can only assist readers to form their own judgment by reprinting two of his articles, HUMANITY FIRST, which I take to be a sincere statement of what he felt; and the THE NEW PARSIFAL, which I take on its face value as being a magnificent piece of leg-pulling:

HUMANITY FIRST
(Reprinted from *The International*, November, 1917.)

It may be that one day the gold plate with its diamond inscriptions may be stripped by some Vandal—Macaulay's New Zealander or another—from my sarcophagus. It may be that centuries later still the learned archæologists of some nation yet unguessed, excavating the ruins of Westminster Abbey may find those bones and send them to anatomists for examination.

The report of these anatomists may be something in these terms: "These are the bones of a mammal, a primate, homo sapiens. The skull is not prognathous; this person was probably a Caucasian."

In such a judgment I acquiesce with pleasure. It would be limitation to be described as "this German," or "this Japanese." Man is man, and in him burns the mystic flame of Godhead. It is a blasphemy to discriminate further, to antithesize the Russian against the Turk, in any matter more serious than national belief, custom, or costume.

All advanced thinkers, all men who realize the divine plan, desire and intend the solidarity of humanity;

and the patriot in the narrow and infuriated sense of that word is a traitor to the true interest of man. It may be necessary, now and the, to defend one's own section of mankind from aggression; but even this should always be done with the mental reservation: "May this war be the nurse of a more solid peace; may this argument lead to a better understanding; may this division lead to a higher union!

A man's worst enemies are those of his own household, and the worst foes of any nation are its petty patriots. "Patriotism is the last resort of scoundrel." The deliberate antagonizing of nations is the foulest of crimes. It is the Press of the warring nations that, by inflaming the passions of the ignorant, has set Europe by the ears. Had all men been educated and travelled, they would not have listened to those harpy-shrieks. Now the mischief is done, and it is for us to repair it as best we may. This must be our motto: "Humanity First."

All persons who generalize about nations: "Germans are murderers"—"Frenchmen are all adulterers"— "Englishmen are all snobs"—"Russians are all drunkards"—and so on, must be silenced. All persons who cling to petty interests and revenges must be silenced. We must refuse to listen to any man who does not realize that civilization itself is at stake, that even now Europe may be so weakened that it may fall a prey to the forces of atavism, that war may be followed by bankruptcy, revolution, and famine, and that even within our own lifetime the Tower of Ages may be fallen into unrecognizable ruins.

We must refuse to listen to any man who has not resolutely put away from him all limited interest, all national passion, who cannot look upon wounded humanity with the broad, clear gaze, passionless and yet compassionate, of the surgeon, or who is not single-minded in his determination to save the life at whatever cost of mutilation to any particular limb.

We must listen most to the German who understands that England is a great and progressive and enlightened nation, whose welfare is necessary to the health of Europe; and the Frenchman who sees in Germany his own best friend, the model of science, organization and foresight, which alone can build up the fallen temple anew. We must listen to the Englishman who is willing to acquiesce in the Freedom of the Seas; and to the Russian who acknowledges that it is time to put a term to the tyranny and corruption of his rules.

The yelping Press of every country, always keen to gather pennies from the passion of the unthinking and unknowing multitude, will call every such man a traitor.

So be it. Let the lower interest be betrayed to the higher, the particular benefit of any given country to the Commonwealth of the whole World. Let us no more consider men, but man. Let us remember who came from heaven and was made flesh among the Jews, not to lead his own people to victory, not to accept that partial dominion of the earth, but to bring light and truth to all mankind.

Had the Savior of Humanity deigned to accept the patriotic mission of driving out Romans, he would have united his nation, but man would not have been redeemed. Therefore his people called him traitor, and betrayed him to their own oppressors.

Let those who are willing, as He was, to accept the opprobrium, need be, the Cross, come forward; let them bear the Oriflamme of the Sun for their banner, for that the Sun Shineth alike upon all nations of the earth; and let them ever flash in the forefront of their battle this one redeeming thought: "Humanity First."

That thought has been the key in which these essays have been written.

Aleister Crowley.

* * * * *

THE NEW PARSIFAL.
A Study of Wilhelm II.
By Aleister Crowley.
(Reprinted from "*The Open Court.*")

World-crises are always preceded by world-prophets. The artist is the secret incarnation of the Zeitgeist; his contemporaries always fail to recognize him even as an artist, unless he live long enough to impose his will upon them, and so see the world swing slowly towards his sun.

I am fortunate in that, young as I still am, I behold the establishment of the moral principles for which I fought even as a boy. I see the death agony of sham religion, the destruction of that cave of petty tyrannies and narrow ideals that the "good" called the "home," the general recognition of what was then called degeneracy, but was in truth moral courage asserting its divine destiny, as part of the normal life of the best men.

Hypocrisy is squirming still, but such is the habit of slain reptiles. So, before I am forty, I find the world almost an ideal place to live in. Being an optimist, I had hoped much; but this greatest thing I had hardly dared to hope, the dissolution of Syphilization in universal war. Only in my prophet-mood could I speak it aloud.

I feel that there is a certain historical importance in making this claim, for the Celtic race, the holy clan that derive even their blood from Osiris and Isis, must constantly deserve the golden harp upon the banner of green, the symbol of poetic inspiration, and the older banner, the sun blaze, which I bear on my own shield, token of the fatherhood of Apollo.

For there were prophets in the shrine before me, and it is of them I speak. The weapon of one was music, of the other philosophy. And these two men understood what was seething in Europe, were torn by the throes of the birth of this giant child of time. Horus, the God of War. And so secret and so awful was this labor that no poet could join their godly company, else it may be the birth had been hasted and the child stillborn. Even now when he is come, he appears in so black a veil that men, remembering the prophet of Khorassan, shudder and pass on.

But after the rule of the prophet comes the rule of the king. In the world-crisis which they foresee arises the hero. And just as they are forced to prophesy against their will, so often enough the hero is a man of peace. Anyone who has studied the history of Napoleon with broad clear vision will not read ambition, but necessity, in his campaigns. The shallow mind forgets that at that time, France, already self-mutilated and bleeding from the revolution, was beset by the armies of the world. Napoleon saved France from Bourbon sloth, stupidity and selfishness in the hour of the ruin they had brought about. His subsequent wars were the fruits of his past victories. If you disturb equilibrium ever so little the whole universe shakes. In order to readjust the machinery which has slipped a single cog, it may sometimes be necessary to scrap the whole plant and rebuild it from new material. It is impossible to localize war. For the moment the affair may be prevented from spreading, but the force continues to operate invisibly.

So by the irony of the gods the warrior king is often a man of peace. The popular mind is unable to perceive these subtleties. It tends to regard Julius Cæsar as a warrior rather than a legislator, and Mohammed to this day is considered rather as the conqueror than as the greatest author and lawgiver of the Christian era, the man who built up a civilization whose essential force carried Europe through the dark ages, and prevented the destruction of knowledge from being complete.

Thus, it being necessary for the popular mind to interpret the prophets in some concrete manner, the popular imagination seizes on some convenient figure and makes him a hero. There he stands, in marble sometimes, more often in bronze, but always with the inscription "Hail, Savior of the world" upon the pedestal.

The lavish gods have matched their prophets well with their hero this time. Wilhelm II* has always been to a certain extent conscious of himself as an incarnation of Lohengrin, Siegfried, Parsifal.

---

* It is remarkable that Franz Josef fit in quite well as the aged King. He is Titurel.

The last thing that Wagner wanted to draw was an overman. Wagner's intellect was socialistic. But the prophet in him, as in every true artist, was aristocratic; and every time he drew, he drew a saviour. His hero was not merely a king, but a holy king. He was the custodian of a sacred treasure; he wielded magic weapons, and wore armour consecrated and invulnerable.

It was a great thing for Germany that she had an emperor with the intelligence to perceive what these things meant, and to realize himself as the Messiah of whom the prophet Wagner spoke. This being so, he stepped readily and naturally into the place, as on a well-rehearsed stage. Already, before the war is ended, he is apparent even to neutrals and to enemies as the central figure of the drama, the new Agamemnon.

This is the age of fairy tales. The newspapers have weaned us from the truth. So even the All-lies have conspired in stupid hate to endow the Kaiser with all the qualities of a demigod. In truth, to his own soldiers he appears, flashing hither and thither, like St. Michael, to rally, to encourage, to lead forward in the charge. Where the fight is thickest, there is the emperor, pale and stern, like Christ as he arose from Gethsemane and walked forth to meet Fate, and to find triumph and immortal glory. From front to front he rages, whirling aloft the consecrated sword of his fathers. He never spares himself; he is a comrade to every soldier in the ranks.

There is something here to catch the popular imagination. To his very enemies he seems like Lucifer or

Attila, not wholly human. They endow him with the magic gifts; he is reported simultaneously on every battle front, as well as in a dozen of his castles. Even the Crown Prince is killed a hundred times and rises to renew the combat, ever more glorious because more glittering as he breaks through the spider-web of myth whose gossamer shrouds him as with the veil of a high priestess over the silver armor of a knight of the Graal.

There is so much magic drapery about the Czar. He is in Petrograd, and goes to the front now and again, a mere king, hardly a warrior kings, certainly not a sacred king, and still less a demi-god. But Wilhelm II is the genius of his people. He has the quality that Castor and Pollux had for Rome. He seems omniscient, omnipotent, omnipresent, the very angel of God, terrible and beautiful, sent to save the Fatherland from savage foes. Even if he perish, he will not perish as a man. He will acquire the radiance of Milton's Satan, and go down the ages as the hero of the great lost cause of humanity.

None will know the place of his burial. Legends will grow up around him as they did for Christ, for Balder, for Adonis, for Arthur, for Mohammed, for Napolean. "He is not really dead; he will come again to lead his people to the final triumph," will be the word in the mouth of every peasant, and a subconscious hope in the heart of every noble. The poet will know that this is mystically true; for he knows that there is no death, that character is more permanent than flesh and blood, that men are in truth the incarnation of some god. He knows that the hero, compact of myth, is yet more real than the historical figure of the man himself. Imagination holds more truth than science; art is real, life is illusion. For art holds the idea complete and pure, the divine though, clothed about with beauty. Art formulates deity; art from the quarries of the amorphous earth, builds its imperishable palace of white marble, or of onyx, porphyry and malachite.

Ave, Guglielme! Rex, imperator! Hail, Savior of the world, that clad in golden armor, with the helm of holiness, wieldest the sword! Hail, sovereign and saviour, that healest all the diseases of the ages, that hurlest back the heathen from the sacred realm.

Welcome to the world that lay in anguish, hungering for thy dawn, O sun of righteousness! The holy kings of old salute thee; the prophets anoint thee with the oil of benediction; they offer thee the crown of Europe. The poets see thee, and know thee; their songs weave silken veils about thine armour!

Ave, Guglielme, rex, imperator!

ACTIVITIES IN AMERICA

For the rest, Crowley in America continued to be active physically and mentally, and to figure from time to time sensationally in the Press, as might be expected.

Upon his arrival in December, 1914, he was "interviewed" by the reporters, who naturally found him good "copy," as the following "story" from the *New York World* exemplifies:

MASTER MAGICIAN REVEALS WEIRD SUPERNATURAL RITES

Aleister Crowley, who recently arrived in New York, is the strangest man I ever met. He is a man about whom men quarrel. Intensely magnetic, he attracts people or repels them with equal violence. His personality seems to breed rumors. Everywhere they follow him.

One man to whom I spoke of him lauded Crowley as a poet of rare delicacy, the author of "Hail Mary," a garland of verses in honour of the Mother of God. Another alluded to him as an unsparing critic of American literature. Another knew him as the holder of some world records for mountain-climbing. Still another warned me against him as a thoroughly bad man, a Satanish or devil-worshipper steeped in black magic, the high priest of Beelzebub. An actor knew him only as a theatrical producer and as a designer of extraordinary stage costumes. A publisher told me that Crowley was an essayist and philosopher whose books, nearly all privately printed, were masterpieces of modern printing. Among his works is a voluminous treatise on the history and practices of magic, representing immense research and erudition—the authoritative book on the subject. By others he was variously pictured to me as a big game hunter, as a gambler, as an editor, as an explorer. Some said he was a man of real attainments, others that he was a faker. All agreed that he was extraordinary....

While in America, he travelled extensively from coast to coast over that vast continent, visiting Florida, New Orleans, Los Angeles, San Francisco and the Middle West, travelling up the Hudson in a canoe, living as a hermit on Œsopus Island—always restless. In New York, he played a number of light-hearted pranks, not the least being the "Declaration of Irish Independence" on July 3rd, 1915, which he proclaimed at the foot of the Statue of Liberty after throwing his "British passport" (an old envelope!) into the river harbour, and making the following portentous speech:

> I have not asked any great human audience to listen to these words; I had rather address them to the unconquerable ocean that surrounds the world, and to the free four winds of heaven. Facing the sunrise, I lift up my hands and my soul herewith to this giant figure of Liberty, the ethical counterpart of the Light, Life and Love which are our spiritual heritage. In this symbolical and most awful act of religion, I invoke the one true God of whom the Sun Himself is but a shadow that He may strengthen me heart and hand to uphold that freedom for the land of my sires, which I am come hither to proclaim.
>
> In this dark moment, before the father orb of our system kindles with his kiss the sea, I swear the great oat of the Revolution.
>
> I tear with my hands this token of slavery, this safe-conduct from the enslaver of my people (does so); I renounce for ever all allegiance to every alien tyrant; I swear to fight to the last drop of my blood to liberate

the men and women of Ireland; and I call upon the free people of this country, on whose hospitable shores I stand an exile, to give me countenance and assistance in my task of breaking these bonds which they broke for themselves 138 years ago.

I proclaim the Irish Republic! I unfurl the Irish flag! Eire go Bragh! God save Ireland!

Another practical joke was "a publicity scheme" which Crowley's fertile brain evolved in order to sell a book written by an acquaintance of his. He inserted about a hundred small advertisements in provincial papers to the effect that a reward of $10,000 would be paid (by the author) to anyone who would recover for him, in its undamaged form, the image of Kwannon which stolen from Sun Yat Sen at Shanghai on June 13th, 1904.

The result was that hundreds of reports and Press photographers, with amateur detectives, besieged the amazed author's house; and at least 600 newspaper "stories," many of them full page, all of them full of the wildest inventions and speculations, appeared in the American Press, until Crowley, thinking the joke had gone far enough, "blew the gaff." Even then, American reports called on the innocent Sun Yat Sen in faraway China, and asked him for *his* side of the story. The President told them, with dignity, that he had lived a long while, and heard a lot about the extravagance of newspaper stories, but never in his life had he yet heard anything so silly!

At the time of Prohibition, Crowley gave in New York a "benzine jag" to which invitations in the following form were issued:

JULY 1st. JOYFUL CELEBRATION!

The Grand Master invites the representatives of the Press, the Prohibition Movement, the Pulpit, Poetry, and the Police to join in the inaugural festival of the BENZINE JAG. 9 p.m. July 1. No. 63 Washington Square. Love is the law, love under will.

One of the "representatives of the Press" ended his description of the "Jag" as follows:

Once out in Washington Square, the visitor took several deep breaths, caught benzine fumes, walked a straight path, thought normally, and wondered, "Where is that benzine jag?"

Yet unquestionably, he had been under the influence of the benzine because, for three hours, he had been glibly conversing on his "inner self" and a rare variety of subjects with which he had heretofore been slightly acquainted. And furthermore he had made several warm friendships under the power of the benzine.

Here is the prescription for the "benzine jag" which doctors say is not harmful if taken in small quantities, Mr. Crowley avers.

Buy an ordinary can of benzine, take a dropper, get capsules, put twenty drops of benzine in each capsule and then take as if it were a pill."

Crowley also became a painter about this time, and made a sensation in Greenwich Village by inserting the following advertisement in the daily Press:

DWARFS, HUNCHBACKS, Tattooed Women, Harrison Fisher Girls, Freaks of All Sorts, Coloured Women, only if exceptionally ugly or deformed, to pose for artist. Apply in letter with photograph. Box 707.

A reporter, visiting his studio, took back a beautiful "story" to his editor:

> I had never studied art and had never drawn or painted a picture in my life. When I tried to draw I became so interested in the work that I gave up the editorship of the magazine and went in for art. What you see around you is the result. What sort of artist am I? Oh, I don't know just what to call myself. I'd say, off-hand, that I was an old master."

THE INTERNATIONAL

Crowley soon transformed this vaguely radical paper. He contributed occasional articles during 1916, but in August 1917, he took control of it entirely, and wrote practically the whole of the contents, under numerous aliases, just as he had done in the days of the EQUINOX. From that time onwards, all vague political theorisings and ponderousness was banished from its pages. Amongst other contributions from Crowley were two really notable series of short stories, SIMON IFF (detective), by "Edward Kelley" and a collection of stories now called GOLDEN TWIGS (from their thematic derivation in Sir J. G. Frazer's "The Golden Bough"), by "Mark Wells" and others—all Aleister Crowley, of course. There was some "popular" exposition of Magick, some poetry, and only occasionally any reference to the Great War (e.g. HUMANITY FIRST). In April 1918, the control of the journal passed out of Crowley's hands into those of one Lindsay M. Keasbey, formerly a professor of Political Science at the University of Texas. The magazine, therefore, became defunct.

THE "EQUINOX" AGAIN

Five years of silence having elapsed (the second volume), Crowley now began to re-issue the EQUINOX ("Vol. 3") in the spring of 1918. The first number appeared, quite up to the standard of the old English days. Number 2 of the volume, I understand, also went to press for the autumn; but financial difficulties prevented Crowley from bringing it out—further significant commentary on the legend of German gold. He therefore abandoned the idea of proselytising any further in America.

In 1919 he returned to Europe.

CROWLEY AND AMERICA

Even before he first visited New York in 1900, the poet had written an APPEAL TO THE AMERICAN REPUBLIC, very adolescent, Swinburnian, and sincere, which was none the less a call for the unity of the English-speaking peoples—amazingly ahead of its time. The poem was published with a cover design of crossed flags—the Union Jack and the Stars and Stripes. Its style and sentiments may be appreciated from the following excerpts:

> Thou fair Republic oversea afar,
>   Where long blue ripples lap the fertile land,
> Whose manifest dominion, like a star,
> Fixed by the iron hands and swords of war,
>   Now must for aye, a constellation, stand—
> Thou new strong nation! as the eagle aspires
>   To match the sun's own fires,
> Children of our land, hear the children of
>   your sires.

* * * * *

The morning of deliverance is at hand;
   The world requickens, and all folk rejoice,
Seeing our kingdom look toward your land,
And both catch hands, indissolubly grand
   In the proud friendship of a better choice.
Your winds that wrought wild wreckage
    on our shore
   Shall sink and be no more,
Or waft your barks, with wheat gold-laden,
    swiftly o'er.

* * * * *

Are not your veins made purple with our blood,
   And our dominions touch they not afield?
Pours not the sea its long exultant flood
On either's coast? The rose has one same bud
   And the vine's heart on purple pledge
    doth yield.
Are we not weary of the fanged pen?
   Are we not friends, and men?
Let us look frankly face to face—and quarrel then!

There was much more in this vein (39 stanzas) and I cannot help thinking that the poem is one of the most significant Crowley documents which I have examined in relation to that portion of his "legend" which whispers "traitor!" [Unless it be that Crowleyan suggestion published in the form of a letter to the *Observer*, of 27th September, 1914, which attracted some attention at the time:

POETIC JUSTICE
(To the Editor of the *Observer.*)

Sir:—

Poetic justice to Rheims is possible. It is well within the power of modern builders to transplant thither Cologne Cathedral, stone by numbered stone. Let this be the symbol and monument of our victory.

—Yours faithfully,

Aleister Crowley.]

His APPEAL TO THE AMERICAN REPUBLIC, with minor alterations only, was reprinted in the *English Review* in October, 1914—his prophetic insight, or perhaps it should be called poetic statesmanship, of fifteen years earlier having then become more readily applicable to current events.

Even then, his appeal for an alliance was not relished by certain literary Englishmen, for example by the critic in the *New Age*, who wrote thus about his poem as reprinted:

> ...One would suppose that that sordid continent has become for Mr. Crowley one of Swinburne's idealized girl-harlots. Did anyone ever hear such language as this addressed to a continent of Yankees intent on capturing German trade in South America while England holds up German shipping at her own cost?

The prophet was certainly without honour in his own land!

However, his lyrical affection for America was tempered by an affectionate prerogative of criticism, instanced by an article which appeared in the *English Review* in November, 1913, entitled ART IN AMERICA. The article attracted a wide attention, both in England and in America. It was severe. The following *précis* of it, which appeared in the *Yorkshire Herald*, may serve to show its general import:

> That remarkable young gentleman, Mr. Aleister Crowley, says some hard things about America in the "English Review." He criticizes the art of the country with a pen that must have laid in vitriol since Byron threw it down. Longfellow, his pop-gun loaded with pop-corn, and Whittier is little better than Moody and Sankey! "Of the Channings, one need only remark that the uncle was a pedant and the nephew an ignoramus." "And there was undoubtedly one Cornelius Matthews, who burst his poetic gun on the first time he fired it." In painting, Mr. Crowley declares that Alex. Harrison painted two passable pictures by accident. America has no music, and the only American sculptor that he knows of is a Lithuanian living in Paris. "The boasted scientific inventions of the Americans do not exist. What they invent is 'notions,' based on the discovery of others. Edison is merely an organizer and adapter of scientific brains." But had you heard of Aleister Crowley?

The Times referred to the article as:

> An entirely preposterous, but quite enjoyable, tirade.

The *Northern Whig* commented:

> An article which should make him a target, not for individuals, but for an outraged nation. Mr. Crowley touches our transatlantic neighbours on their weakest spot by proclaiming that their boasted culture is a pose. ...His judgments certainly do not err on the side

of leniency.... One could understand American patriots clamouring for President Wilson to suppress Mr. Crowley as he has tried to suppress Gen. Huerta.

The *Academy* evoked memories of Wild West films:

> Aleister Crowley has an article on "Art in America" which should set all Americans who own to pride of country hot on his trail with loaded revolvers.

—while the *New York Evening Post* attempted to be aristocratically superior:

> If America can be ridiculed for its average tourist, it at least furnishes nothing quite so humorous as the type of omniscience here illustrated.... The article reflects the opinions of a considerable number of Englishmen, especially of the so-called lower middle class.

It follows from this incident that Crowley, in going to America to live during the War, had undoubtedly a sincere enough desire to advocate a union between England and America in the world crisis; but it also follows that the was bound to rub self-conscious Americans the wrong way, thinking as he did that they were culturally backward. I would hazard the suggestion that, whereas his earlier extensive travels in the East had isolate the poet spiritually from the English quagmire, his war-time sojourn and extensive travellings in the West did something to make him realise that England, with its traditions, after all, was at least not so detestable as once he had thought. This is merely my surmise. If he came back to England in 1919 in that spirit he was rapidly to be disillusioned by the reception which was awaiting him at the hands of James Douglas and Bottomley's successors, more barbarous and hysterical than the wildest extravagances he might have deplored in "uncultured" America.

AFTER THE WAR

CHAPTER V

After The War

The question might well be asked, *Why* did James Douglas and the *Sunday Express* and Bottomley's successors on *John Bull* select Crowley as an object of their unrestrained and indescribably slanderous vituperation? The campaign against him was a severity unexampled in the history of English journalism in that a private individual was its butt. During the War the Kaiser, and immediately after the War, Lenin and Trotsky, were reviled and execrated in terms of opprobrious hyperbole exceeding the limits of sane imagination. But these were public individuals, personifications of "Hunnishness" and "Bolshevism," and the propaganda attacks upon them were part of a calculated policy. They were symbols, not persons. But Aleister Crowley was attacked as a person, and not as the personification of any policy or idea. The technique of propaganda, perfected against "Hunnishness" and "Bolshevism," was now employed, holus-bolus, to discredit an English man of letters.

Is it fantastic to suggest the following possible explanation of the campaign against Crowley?—That during the War Fleet Street had been trained, especially by Northcliffe, in the technique of scientific propaganda which may be defined as personal vituperation based on moral horror; that after

Versailles, it was no longer necessary to vituperate the Kaiser, but that Lenin and Trotsky were easily to hand as substitutes, and that the vituperative weapon was sharpened still further upon their bodies; but that after the failure of Allied strike of British workmen (1921) against intervention in Russia, the "Bolshevik menace" propaganda began to lose its point; and that nevertheless a whole generation of specialist vituperative writers had to "carry on" in Fleet Street somehow.

We may presume, not only that the copywriters of Fleet Street were trained in the School of Propagandist Abuse, but that their postulate millions of readers had also become accustomed to expect this kind of thing. Crowley came into the news opportunity for journalists confronted with a dearth of "horrors." The rusting weapons of vituperation were polished and brought into play. Such is an hypothesis.

To the credit nevertheless of British journalism, whatever excesses may have been committed during the War and the Bolshevik revolution, only two journals, the *Sunday Express* and *John Bull*, failed to distinguish between vituperation of a public and a private individual. Amongst all the newspapers and journals in Fleet Street, *only these two* attacked and "exposed" Aleister Crowley. This fact is a tribute to the decency and restraint of Fleet Street in general, where the important power of publicity must be constantly regarded as a power to be used with the utmost discretion, particularly when the publicity is to be adverse, and against a private individual.

Nevertheless, the two papers just mentioned as an exception were "important" and widely circulated. The attack which they launched was potentially and actually quite different in effect from what had hitherto been the worse newspaper defamation of Crowley—the miserable *Looking Glass* affair of

1910. This latter Crowley had ignored as being too trivial to bother about, as indeed it was, had the line then initiated by De Wend Fenton not been developed by James Douglas and *John Bull* within more recent memory. Then, he was unwilling to defend himself by recourse to the processes of Law; even had he won a libel action against the Looking Glass there was more than a considerable doubt whether the company or its editor would have had the assets to pay reasonable damages. Now, the wealth of the papers defaming him was so colossal as to put it beyond the shadow of a doubt that they would have been able to pay substantial damages, if Crowley had secured a verdict. But, by the same token, they would have been able to command legal resources for their defence immeasurably greater than anything Crowley would have been able to command for their prosecution. He was without money, he was sick, he was in a foreign country. They launched their attack in an immunity from legal consequences quite as effective as if they had been attacking the Huns or the Bolsheviks. By a curious irony, only two kinds of newspapers can afford to defame an individual—those with scarcely any assets, and those with enormous reserves. Moreover, the safest way to libel an individual is to pile on the infamy so thick, to make the allegations so fantastic and numerous, that they become impossible to refute by the canons of common sense which regulate trial by jury. *John Bull*, for example, said that Crowley was a cannibal. How could he prove to a British jury that he was not a cannibal? Particularly when at the same time he was accused of all kinds of "unmentionable" vice? Even a stupid barrister would have no difficulty in proving to a jury that Crowley is not a Christian. Moreover, that he is actively opposed to the practice and ethics of Christianity. There is enormous prejudice No. 1.

After that, many jurymen would have no difficulty in believing that he was a cannibal. And Crowley had no possible means, in logic or in evidence, of *proving the contrary!* Consider, too, the effect that would be produced upon a jury of good men and true who were asked to examine, in the course of a trial, the writings of Aleister Crowley, which would undoubtedly be admitted as evidence! We have seen how those works puzzled even sophisticated critics. What effect would they have upon a jury asked to examine marked passages? So much prejudice would be created by them that Crowley would have the greatest difficulty in exonerating himself from the grosser charges.

I go at some length into the psychology, as I conceive it, of those who conducted the campaign against Crowley in order to answer the doubts of many people, otherwise quite friendly to the poet, who nevertheless ask insistently: *Why did he not take action?* The fact that Crowley is a literary man places him in an abnormal category, because the writings of a literary man are always admissible in evidence of his character. Indeed, such is literature. Nevertheless there is an injustice in submitting a literary man, through his works, to the ordeal of estimation by a jury; however admirable in other respects the jury system may be. A literary man, above all a poet, seldom writes "down" to the appreciation of average "good men and true." Despite this, he may be a great writer. So much is almost a platitude, yet I must insist upon its importance as an explanation of Crowley's motives in *not* defending himself at law against the attacks which appeared in the *Sunday Express* and *John Bull*.

The poet's revenge upon his detractors is slow. Byron was savagely attacked during his lifetime. Who attacked him? Was it James Douglas in a previous incarnation? Nobody knows. I venture to suppose that long after the present James Douglas is defunct and forgotten, some of the men and ideas he has attacked will be living and remembered. If only because he has attacked D. H. Lawrence and Aleister Crowley, James Douglas will go to oblivion. Such is the poet's revenge.

I select Douglas for this mention because it was Douglas who initiated the attack upon Crowley with a "review" of THE DIARY OF A DRUG FIEND, written in that pious and shuddering idiom of his which has nowadays become more familiar, and less significant, than then it was. *John Bull* merely followed a lead given by the *Sunday Express*, as previously it had merely followed a lead given by the *Looking Glass*.

John Douglas called for the suppression of THE DIARY OF A DRUG FIEND in November, 1922. His splash headline was "A Book for Burning." His copywriters made a sensational front-page "news" splash the following week, in order to bring extra pressure upon the publishers, in the recognised manner of the Fleet Street potentate at work "getting things done." This attack reached the utmost violence of which vituperative journalism is capable. The following Spring there was a continuation of the "exposures" following the death of Raoul Loveday at Cefalù. Then the "story" fizzled.

And the damage had been done, though only the notoriously silly *John Bull* kept the story going, or even took any notice of the story, amongst all English journalism. I do not mean to pay James Douglas a compliment when I say that he really showed some power in his campaign against Aleister Crowley. At least partly because of the *Sunday Express* allegations, Crowley was "expelled" from Fascist Italy, and later from France. This is a use of power, undoubtedly. It is also a superb example of the abuse of power, abuse of the prerogative of defending "public interest" which is supposed to be in the hands of the Press.

I have stated very plainly that I think Crowley has often acted foolishly in the course of his adventurous life. I cannot believe that he has acted criminally. If he has acted criminally, Scotland Yard should take action, now that he is living in England. Will James Douglas take this up again, and clear up the uncertainty one way or another? He will not.

And if James Douglas and the *Sunday Express* will not now make the attempt to have Crowley put in prison, will they, on the other hand, retract, or do anything to correct, misstatements made at the time which are demonstrably false, and of which the following is a typically pernicious example:

(Extract from article entitled: "Aleister Crowley's Orgies in Sicily"—November 26th, 1922)
WOMEN VICTIMS

Three women he keeps there permanently for his orgies. All of them he brought from America two or three years ago. One is a French-American governess, one is an ex-schoolmistress, and one a cinema actress from Los Angeles.

Whenever he needs money, and cannot get it from fresh victims, he sends them on the streets of Palermo or Naples to earn it for him.

He served once a prison sentence in America for procuring young girls for a similar purpose.

It will be observed that these statements accuse Crowley, not only of being a criminal, but of being a convicted felon. Three women who are identifiable are accused of having been prostitutes. It would be supposed that no responsible editor would publish such statements without being able fully to substantiate them.

What are the facts? How could such allegations as these be refuted in a court of Law?

The onus of proof should be on the newspaper making the allegation. It is unfair to ask an accused person to establish a negative, particularly when the allegation is preposterous. The definite statement that Crowley has been in prison is, however, of another order. It should be possible to give the date and place, together with full particulars of the charge, from official records.

Unless this can be done, the statement is a gross and filthy lie and libel. I am assured that, not only has Crowley never been in prison, but he has never even been accused of any crime before any court in any country of the world.

Even at this late date, will the *Sunday Express* either prove or withdraw the allegation? I wonder! In the meantime, may we not presume Crowley innocent until he is proved otherwise before the proper tribunal? Such is, of course, the cornerstone of English judicial procedure. And if Crowley should happen to be innocent, then what shall be said of the editor of the *Sunday Express*? The whole matter certainly needs investigation.

* * * * *

We must now pass, restraining nausea, to a consideration of the actual documents in accordance with the only certain procedure of redress at present open.

Before reprinting the article by James Douglas which started the "mud-ball" rolling, an opinion as to THE DIARY OF A DRUG FIEND might be formed from the three following reviews in representative papers. These reviews are quoted in full:

The Times Literary Supplement. November 16, 1922.

Mr. Crowley has not the literary fascination of a De Quincey or the power and stark realism of a Zola. His most conspicuous gift is an effervescent imagination, an exuberant diction; and in the rhapsodies, despairs, and regeneration of Sir Peter and Lady Pendragon, ardent devotees of cocaine and "heroin," retailed in a "Paradiso" (by Sir Peter), an Inferno (by his wife), and a "Purgatorio" (by Sir Peter), we certainly do not reach, though he avers it to be a "true story," any impression of a real human experience. They roam about Paris and Europe, palpitating at first with "internal ecstasy and the intoxicating sense that the whole world admired and envied us." They "had sprung in on leap to be coterminous with the Universe," and so on; then they sank into "boundless bliss" but drifting "down the dark and sluggish river of inertia towards the stagnant, stinking morass of insanity"; and through the horror of despair they reach at last the Abbey of Thelema, where diminution of does and dissertations on life and its meanings, control of the will, and the 'credo' of a Gnostic and Catholic Church of Light, Life, Love and Liberty give them mastery of the will and of degenerating emotion; and the belief that there is nothing in nature, even drugs, which cannot be used for our benefit. The book teems both with an immense fertility of incidents and idea; and with an amazingly rich crop of rhetoric. It is impossible to say that at any moment in the career of Peter and his wife do we seem to be in touch with reality. It is all a phantasmagoria of ecstasies, despairs, and above all verbiage.

The Observer.   *December 10, 1922.*

"I got another packet and put it in my mouth. He went wild and clutched me by the hair, and forced open my jaws with his finger and thumb. I struggled and kicked and scratched, but he was too strong. He got it out and put it in his own mouth. Then he hit me in the face as I sat." This extract is from the diary of a young woman who has the cocaine habit. As she starts by chanting "O thou fragrance of sweet flowers, that art wafted over blue fields of air! I adore thee, Evoe! I adore thee, I.A.O.!" there seems a slightly falling off in her style—which only goes to bear out the argument of the whole and to show that these good drugs, as masters, do not exactly improve the manners, whatever they may do as servants. Mr. Crowley suddenly leaves these slightly disgusting surroundings, and removes his young people to a wondrous place of treatment mainly by addresses and incantation. He declares that the place exists on this carnal globe, and is willing to act as intermediary should any reader habitually breakfast on heroin and desire to return to bacon and eggs. There is a certain compelling power about the descriptions of degradation. They have a truer ring than the ultra-fantastic patches—although these are credible enough as a rough translation into the speech of every day from a language only heard and understood under frightful and inhuman, if ecstatic, conditions.

The Daily Herald.   *November 15, 1922.*

Drug-taking, to judge from *The Diary of a Drug Fiend* (by Aleister Crowley, Collins. 7s. 6d.) seems singularly uninteresting. But, then, I happen most emphatically to dislike losing control over my mental faculties, and the great attraction of drugs appears to be the creation in the mind of false sensation of wonderful power and pleasure—until the virtue goes out of them and they produce no effect whatever, save a restless craving, unless doses are taken regularly.

The one excuse for writing such a book as this is that it should hold out some hope to the victims of this vice; and this Aleister Crowley does, describing the theories, way of living, and scenery of a spot to which the hero-villain and heroine-villainess go, to be brought back to sanity by the discovery of their true work in life.

It is not a pleasing book, but Mr. Crowley invites anyone interested in the system of training he describes to communicate with him. Doubtless there must be many victims, and relatives of victims, of this and other crazes who will accept his invitation.

It seems fairly obvious from these reviews that the book was considered, at its face value, as being a warning against drugs, and an indication of the methods of mental discipline by which the "habit" could be overcome.

James Douglas, however, almost became delirious, drugged himself with morbidity, when he read the book. His "splash" was as follows:

A BOOK FOR BURNING
By James Douglas
(Sunday Express, November 19, 1922)

Some time ago, when our highbrows, or, as they area pleased to call themselves, our intelligentsia, were all praising James Joyce's "Ulysses," I ventured to put it in the pillory as the pinnacle and apex of lubricity and obscenity. But the praise of our highbrows has made it possible for a respectable publisher to hurl into the British home a novel which is modelled upon that scabrous outrage. There are two methods of dealing with pornographic fiction. One is to ignore it lest publicity should inflate its sales. The other method is to raise public opinion so effectively that the book is either withdrawn from circulation by the publisher or is confiscated by public authority.

The Liberty of Art

There is much to be said for the first method. No critic out to puff a vile book by advertising its vileness. Moreover, no critic ought to narrow the liberty of literature or fetter the art of the artist. If there be a doubt, freedom ought to be given the benefit. On the other hand, if pornographic novels are ignored they tend to become more pornographic. They quickly expand their licence. The effect upon young writers is injurious, for they are tempted to mistake salacity for modernity, obscenity for daring, indecency for independence. Thus the art of the artist is doubly damaged. When the public revolt against the revolting, all artists are tarred with the same brush. The liberty of art is unreasonably curtailed. The pendulum swings from the extreme of licence to the extreme of prudery. And the profession of letters is smirched and soiled by its association with moral lepers.

Ecstatic Eulogy

I have therefore determined to adopt the second method, and to do my best to secure the immediate extirpation of "The Diary of a Drug Fiend" (Collins 7/6 net) by Aleister Crowley. It is a novel describing the orgies of vice practiced by a group of moral degenerates who stimulate their degraded lusts by doses of cocaine and heroin. Although there is an attempt to pretend that the book is merely a study of the depravation caused by cocaine, in reality it is an ecstatic eulogy of the drug and of its effects upon the body and mind. A cocaine trafficker would welcome it as a recruiting agent which would bring him thousands of new victims.

Cunning Blasphemies

The characters of the novel are repulsive....The gospel preached by the book is this: "Do what thou wilt shall be the whole of the law." The obscenities are flavoured with cunning blasphemies....

There is even a parody of the Creed. At the baser and more bestial horrors of the book it is impossible, even if it were desirable, to hint.

It may be asked how such a book could secure a publisher. Well, few publishers have time to read the books which they publish, and even their readers sometimes read them hastily. I imagine that this book secured publication in the guise of an exposure of the evils wrought by drugs. But its true character is stamped on it in spite of its ingenious use of innuendo and artifice. It is a book that ought to be burned. Why lock up cocaine-traffickers if we tolerate cocaine novels?

In order to second this virtuous attempt to secure "the same immediate extirpation" of the novel, the *Sunday Express* followed up, a week later, with a front page story, here reprinted *in extenso*:

> *Sunday Express.*   *November 26, 1922.*
> ### COMPLETE EXPOSURE OF "DRUG FIEND" AUTHOR
> BLACK RECORD OF ALEISTER CROWLEY
> Preying on the Debased.
> His Abbey.
> Profligacy and Vice in Sicily.
>
> The "Sunday Express" last week demanded the suppression of a book, "The Diary of a Drug Fiend," written by a person called Aleister Crowley.
>
> "At the baser and more bestial horrors of the book it is impossible to hint," wrote Mr. James Douglas.
>
> The publishers state that it is their intention to push the sales of this pernicious work.
>
> The "Sunday Express" was determined that the public should be protected, and made the fullest investigations into the career of the author.
>
> *These investigations have produced the most astounding revelations.*
>
> The man Aleister Crowley is the organizer of societies for pagan orgies.
>
> He engaged in pro-German propaganda during the war.
>
> He published obscene attacks on the King.
>
> He made a dramatic renunciation of his British birthright.

He proclaimed himself "King of Ireland."

He stole money from a woman.

He now conducts an "Abbey" in Sicily.

He was in London a month ago, unknown to any except his small circle of intimates.

This is the man whose latest work is a deliberate symposium of obscenity, blasphemy, and indecency.

Man of Many Names

His picture was painted in 1911 by Augustus John, and this year by Jacob Kramer. The latter picture is now on exhibition in London, entitled, "The Beast 666"—which is how the artist saw him.

The "Sunday Express" in reiterating its demand for the withdrawal from circulation of this volume, feels certain that these revelations will induce the publishers—a firm of high repute—to reconsider their decision.

The following is the full life history and record of this sinister author:—

Aleister—formerly Alistair—Crowley was a notorious character in London before the war. He had several aliases which he used on various occasions, including A. E. Crawley, Count von Zonaref, Alastair McGregor, and Earl of Middlesex.

He was, according to his own statement, born at Leamington on October 12, 1875, and is reported to be the son of a Kentish brewer. He is further stated to have studied at Trinity College, Cambridge, in 1896.

"Isis Worship"

Crowley is an author and journalist by profession, and a poet, in spite of the morbidity and perversity of his work, of undoubted accomplishment. His underground activities are less avowable. He came under the notice of the police in 1900 when he stole £200 from a widow with whom he cohabited; the woman, however, refused to prosecute. According to his own statement, Crowley was exploring in Kashmir in 1902 under the auspices of the Austrian Government.

He reappeared in 1903, when he married at Strathpeffer a young widow, Mrs. Skerrett, formerly Miss Rose Kelly; he then called himself McGregor of Boleskine. After this Crowley went to Paris, where he celebrated what he called "Isis Worship." His wife divorced him, and he subsequently married a violinist named Leila Waddell.

The uncleaner forms of occultism, pursued as a means of making money, have been Crowley's chief interest from his early days. He has made various unsuccessful efforts to get recognized by the English Freemasons. He organized an association known as the A.A. (Atlantean Adepts), and later became a member of a Rosicrucian Society, known as the O.T.O. (Ordo Templi Orientis).

His adepts begin every letter and conversation with the greeting, "Do what thou wilt is the whole of the law" (evidently suggested by Rabelais' "Fay ce que voudrais"), and end up "Love is the law, Love under will."

In 1910 Crowley was holding meetings at the Caxton Hall to witness the performance of the "Rites of Eleusis"; he cultivated an immoral society for the worship of the god Pan; and he organized every kind of evil rite including the "Cult of the Beetle" and the Black Mass.

A PRO-GERMAN—

The outbreak of the war put an end to Crowley's activities in England. In November, 1914 Crowley went to the United States, where he entered into close relations with the pro-German propagandists. He edited the New York "International," a German propagandist paper run by the notorious George Silvester Viereck, and published, among other things, an obscene attack on the King and a glorification of the Kaiser.

Crowley ran occultism as a side line, and seems to have been known as the "Purple Priest." Later on he publicly destroyed his British passport before the Statue of Liberty, declared in favour of the Irish Republican cause, and made a theatrical declaration of "war" on England. According to another version of this story, he proclaimed himself at the same time "King of Ireland."

—AND REVOLUTIONARY

During his stay in America Crowley was associated with a body known as the "Secret Revolutionary Committee" which was working for the establishment of the Irish Republic. He is known also as the writer of a defeatist manifesto circulated in France in 1915.

Crowley arrived in France at the beginning of 1920, and subsequently went to Cefalù, Sicily. Here he was head of a community of kindred spirits established at the Villa Santa Barbara, renamed by them "Ad Spiritum Sanctum." Free sexual intercourse seems to have been one of the tenets.

HIS BOOKS

Crowley came back to London this year and settled himself in Chelsea. He goes about garbed usually in a tartan kilt and wearing a black glengarry cap.

Crowley is the author of numerous books, both in verse and prose. Some of these works have typical titles, such as "Alice—An Adultery," "Jezebel," "The God Hater," "Rosa Inferni." At one time he was running a bulky magazine called the "Equinox," addressed to his adepts and embellished with cabalistic signs and photographs from the nude in very doubtful taste.

His portrait was painted in 1911 by Augustus John.

This was not all by any means. There was another full column and a half, including the allegations about white slavery already quoted. There was a story about his "last visit" to London, including the following "interview" with a woman, who lived "in a fashionable quarter":

> I thought that Crowley was simply expounding a theory based on the necessity of one's knowing oneself well.
>
> Even now, I do not understand all his ideas, but I realized how objectionable they must be by a series of pictures he put up in his room. Unspeakably vile things, depicting antique orgies and dreadful vices. He gave a couple of lectures in my house, but I was out on both occasions. He sent out his invitations in the name of "The Master Therion."

* * * * *

I went away for a few days; the man's presence made my own home intolerable to me. In my absence he had an intimation through some source that the police authorities knew of his presence. He at once packed up and went. I understand that he stayed for a few nights at a Turkish bath establishment in the West End before leaving the country.

In a pause for breath before continuing to quote this extravaganza, I hope I am correct in assuming that a mere reprinting of the stuff, more than seven years later, will reveal from internal evidence its nonsensical, distorted and hysterical character. The question arises, Did the journalist who wrote this have his tongue in his cheek, or was he sincere and a moron? I am inclined to deduce that he was merely a clever journalist, extremely able to extract the utmost possible sensation from a story. Given the job of "writing up" Aleister Crowley in a sensational manner, he carried out his instructions ruthlessly. The morality of his procedure is another question, if we remember always that the whole concoction was brewed about a private individual, whose private life was "investigated." How many of us could survive a similar investigation, carried out by journalists trained in denunciation and in the colourful phrase? What would be the private "sexual" record of most other poets and artists, not to mention bankers and commercial travellers? This thought is worth bearing in mind all the time as we go over the indictments against Crowley. He is an exceptional man in many ways, his life has been more full of colour than that of most people. But if any one of us more ordinary persons wrote a book to which James Douglas took exception, and if the *Sunday Express* decided to "expose" us (having first made sure that we would be beyond the reproach of the columnist? How many English villas in Italy or on the Riviera could tell a tale! It was Crowley's predilection for religious ceremonial which gave the bright stunt writer his greatest opportunity:

> The story of the bestial orgies conducted by Aleister Crowley in Sicily sounds like the ravings of a criminal lunatic, made mad by his own depravity, and was related yesterday to the "Sunday Express" representative by a woman who has just returned from the place to London.
>
> The orgies are carried on as mystic religious rites in an old farmhouse near the village of Cefalù, in Sicily. The main room of the house is windowless, with a flagged stone floor. On the floor is painted a great orange circle, lined with pale yellow. Inside the circle are interlaced black triangles. The room is lighted by candles.
>
> ### BURNT INCENSE
> A tripod, upheld by three little fauns, burns incense made of burnt goat's blood and honey. In a cupboard are heaps of little cakes, all made of goats' blood, honey and grain, some raw, and some baked. The raw ones, gone bad, fill the room with a stench.
>
> In this room are carried on unspeakable orgies, impossible of description. Suffice it to say that they are horrible beyond the misgivings of decent people.

How far is a devotee of one religion a credible witness when he describes practices (which he has not seen) of the heathen? The rabid Protestant Evangelical believes that "Maria Monk" is a faithful description of the "goings-on" in Roman Catholic Convents!

But—after all—the attack was following up a denunciation by Mr. James Douglas of a book. And the title of the book was, THE DIARY OF A DRUG FIEND. Consequently:

> Many women come to Cefalù, all with money, for whatever else Crowley may demand of them, money is his primary need. It takes money to supply him with the drugs he uses incessantly, the hashish, cocaine, heroin, opium, morphine, every drug known from the Orient to the Occident.

The theme seems to have wandered away from literary criticism. However, this was rectified in the conclusion of the article:

> What is the literary record of this Mr. Crowley?
>
> Mr. Aleister Crowley is the author of a number of books, most them printed privately. His work, considered as a whole, is a blend of blasphemy, filth, and nonsense. The nonsense is flavoured with mysticism. A very small knowledge of pathology enables one to label him as a well-known type.
>
> As an example of his ideas, one may take the dedication to "Why Jesus Wept"; "To any unborn child, who may learn by the study of this drama to avoid the good and choose the evil, i.e., as judged by Western or Christian standards."
>
> ### REVOLTING POEMS
>
> The numerous allusions to a kind of vague Buddhistic mysticism are clothed in sensuality. Most of the poems are pornographic, many of them revolting, and all of them the product of a diseased mind and a debased character.

In the middle of a long poem called "Alice: an Adultery" there appears this note: "The editor regrets that he is unable to publish this verse." The titles of his books are, for the most part, either biblical or sexual: "Jepthah," "Jezebel," "Aceldama," "The Honourable Adulteress."

Through all his works runs a loathing of Christianity, and he pays Mr. G. K. Chesterton the compliment of a personal attack on him, as one of the last champions of that outworn creed.

He has written on ceremonial magic, and on the state known as "Ecstasy," which relieves one from the dullness and monotony of a normal life. "My mind is pregnant with mad moons and suns," he writes in one place.

All the time he is obsessed with sex and sexual images.

A large number of his books are printed privately—some of them in Paris. They are either incomprehensible or disgusting—generally both. His language is the language of a pervert and his ideas are negligible.

I think that is enough to show the quantity and quality of the abuse with which these unscrupulous journalists reviled the poet. There has never been anything like it in literary history—probably because there has never been anything in literary history like modern sensational journalism. How would the *Sunday Express* have "exposed" Byron? In what terms would they have described "Don Juan," and with what phrases would they have gloated over his amours? What would have been the results if the private life of Shelley and Keats had been dragged into the front page of a Sunday newspaper specialising in moral indignation and invective? Supposing a James Douglas had attacked "Gulliver's Travels" and the relations between Dean Swift and Esther had been "exposed" in a front-page story on the following Sunday!

We must not completely lose our heads, merely because we happen to live in the twentieth century. The treatment accorded to Crowley by his contemporaries may be of some use if it serves us as a warning against the possible dangers peculiar to the age in which we live. Probably there will not be any more unsupportably vile scurrility of this kind. Crowley happened to be the first and worst victim of an abuse of the power of publicity, so enormously inflated during the War, and since the days of million-circulations. If the *Sunday Express* had followed up James Douglas's attack upon "The Well of Loneliness" with columns of violent personal abuse of Miss Radclyffe Hall, public opinion would have been revolted, not by the authoress, but by the newspaper. Nowadays, the *Sunday Express* follows up James Douglas much more carefully, and with much more reserve. We can only assume that Crowley was unfortunate in having been selected as the first and last victim of a policy which is manifestly not allowable, even on the canon of sensational journalism. But what recourse has he? Will the *Sunday Express*, even now, admit that it went too far in this instance? I wonder.

"THE GIRL-WIFE"

Betty May is a charming little lady, very well known in London artistic and "Bohemian" circles. She has had an interesting life. In her Autobiography recently published, she tells of her birth in Limehouse, in sordidly picturesque surroundings, and of her domicile, as a very small child, in sophisticated places such as a Thames barge. Growing up, she longed for a "bigger life" and left the East End and began to earn her living as an artist's model, frequenting the happy-go-lucky Café Royal for many years before and during the War. At one time she went to Paris and joined a gang of Apaches, amongst whom she was known as "Tiger Woman." Returning to England, she was married twice, becoming a widow and divorcee in turn. All this was long before she met Aleister Crowley. Her first husband was a drug addict, and Betty in due course also had given herself up to the habit:

> Even then I had been taking about one hundred grains—ten is a fatal dose to an unaccustomed person—of cocaine per day, varied occasionally with injections of morphia, and my mind and body had already suffered the inevitable effects. I was a victim to morbid suspicious mania, and frequently tried to commit suicide on the most absurd grounds.
>
> (TIGER WOMAN: My Story. By Betty May; Duckworth, 1929. Page 107.)

She promised her second husband that she would "give up taking drugs or spirits during his absence" (at the Front).

> I did not keep this promise. I could not. I used to come across old friends of mine with whom I had gone to dope parties, and gradually the temptation to enjoy the excitement of drugs and the fact that I was lonely became too much for me and I began to take to drugs again. Roy returned one day to find me recovering from a dope party, which had lasted three days and

> three nights. He took off his Sam Browne belt and gave me the severest beating with it I have ever had, which aroused me from my coma into which I had fallen. It was dreadful. I shudder even now when I think of it.
>
> *(idem, p. 113-4.)*

Later, she was divorced from this "he-man" and in due course married Raoul Loveday, while the latter was still an undergraduate at Oxford. Loveday was interested in the occult. This interest had led him to make friends with Aleister Crowley. It should be evident from Betty's own account that she was very much a woman of the world, to put it mildly, long before she had ever met Crowley. I am obliged to draw attention to this fact, not in order to discredit Betty, who is a charming little lady and deservedly popular in "Bohemia" to this day, but in order to enable the reader to understand the reality underlying the subsequent campaign against Crowley which made play of Betty's youth and innocence, left alone with "The Beast" after her husband's death at Cefalù. Betty, it will be gathered, was and is well able to look after herself in any situation, however remarkable or tragic.

Loveday was anxious to study the Occult under Crowley's tuition. He was prepared to act as Crowley's secretary at Cefalù in order to carry out this plan. In October, 1922, Crowley wrote to him in the following terms:

> I hope you will come p.d.q. and bring Betty. I honestly tell you that the best hope for your married life is to get out of the sordid atmosphere of "Bohemian" London. I was really disgusted the other night at the Harlequin. Your songs were good—but what an audience! You are an Oxford man and you don't want your wife in a corner throned on a pile of ordure.

It is ridiculous to knock people down for continuing their old programme. When Betty married a decent man, she should have cut that crowd with a sharp knife. Also, you should have see to it that she did so....

Excuse me playing the Heavy Father; but I like you both so much that I hate to think of the catastrophe which I can see just round the corner. You are both of you accustomed to a certain amount of comfort and decency: and—how does Keats begin Part II of Lamia? At this moment, under the influence of Love, Betty can break with the gluey past. But you must give her a chance to breathe fresh air, and live a clean life. Cefalù represents that chance.

Does it surprise you that the notoriously wicked, A.C. should write thus? If so, you have not understood that he is a man of brutal commonsense, and a loyal friend. So come and live in the open air amid the beauty of Nature.... Beak Street and Fitzroy Street are horrors unthinkable even in Rome; and Rome is a cesspool compared to Cefalù....

The society of Scholars, of free women, and of delightful children will indeed be a great change for Betty; but it is what she needs most. There is in her not only a charming woman, but a good one; and she will develop unsuspected glories, given a proper environment. In London she has not one single decent influence, except your own; and however deeply and truly she may love you, she won't be able to resist "la nostalie de la boue" for ever....

(from original letter in Crowley's files).

Accordingly, Loveday and Betty left London for Cefalù in November, 1922. In February, 1923, Raoul Loveday was dead.

Betty returned to London, was interviewed by *Sunday Express* reporters, and that newspaper again took up the attack upon Crowley, running front-page principal "stunt" articles for two weeks in succession, in the manner of the previous attacks, but more violent even.

Before considering these, it will be well to examine Betty May's most recent account of her husband's death, printed in TIGER-WOMAN (at page 185). Whatever she may have told the reporters at the time, or whatever the reporters may have reported that she told them, this seems to be her considered version of the facts:

> ...When he got steadily worse and a doctor was summoned I found out that he was suffering from enteric, a not uncommon disease in those parts. It was then that I remembered how he had almost certainly caught this disease. One day the Mystic had told Raoul and me to go off for an expedition together. He was in one of his kindly moods and he said Raoul needed some relaxation. He suggested that we should go to a marvellous monastery about thirteen miles off, where the monks would entertain us with food. But he warned us of one thing, which was on no account to touch any water.
>
> We were both delighted. We started off. It was one of the most wonderful days I have seen. We went to the monastery, where the monks gave us bread and soup and showed us all over it. On the way back the heat was appalling. We were both so thirsty that we did not know what to do. Suddenly we came to a mountain spring, bubbling up out of the ground. It was an awful temptation. I do not think that at that time either of us

realized how important it was not to touch the water. Although the Mystic had done his best to impress on us the dangers of drinking, the spring looked so cool and fresh and pure that Raoul could not resist. He knelt down and drank, but in spite of my thirst I managed to restrain myself, though with great difficulty. I suppose I saved my own life. Anyway, I am certain that this is how Raoul caught the disease. He was at once given the right treatment, but no improvement was effected, and he sank fast....

There is no means of ascertaining whether the details of this story are any more exact than the details attributed to Betty by the *Sunday Express* reporters who "interviewed" her. What matters is that Crowley is now completely absolved from the damaging slander of having caused Loveday's death, directly or indirectly. Everything was above board, even to proper medical supervision, and that's that. Now to the muck-throwing in the *Sunday Express*:

> *The Sunday Express.*   *February 25, 1923.*
>
> NEW SINISTER RELATIONS
> OF ALEISTER CROWLEY.
> 'VARSITY LAD'S DEATH.
> Enticed to "Abbey."
> Dreadful Ordeal of a Young Wife.
> Crowley's Plans.
>
> The revelation in the "Sunday Express" recently of obscene orgies carried on by Aleister Crowley—"The Beast 666," as he styles himself—in his "abbey" at Cefalù, Sicily, have been followed by a sinister and tragic happening.

Information has just reached this newspaper of his two latest victims. One of them, a brilliant young English university man, a writer, is dead.

His young wife, a beautiful girl prominent in London artistic circles, arrived in London two days ago in a state of collapse. She is unable to give more than a hint of the horrors from which she escaped.

Worse Horrors Still

She said, however to a "Sunday Express" representative yesterday that the story of Aleister Crowley's sexual debauches and drug orgies are published in this newspaper far understated the real horror of the life in the "abbey" at Cefalù, where he keeps his women and practices his black magic.

This young girl, whose name and that of her husband the "Sunday Express" withholds in deference to the parents' sorrow, said that Crowley offered her husband a secretarial post last autumn when in London. The Beast is possessed of a persuasive smile and suave manners. The young couple had no idea of the true character of the place to which he was inviting them. As the offer seemed to mean travel and congenial work the young husband—a boy of twenty-two—accepted it.

Once they were in Sicily, however, they found they had been trapped in an inferno, a maelstrom of filth and obscenity. Crowley's purpose was to corrupt them both to his own ends.

They resisted him and his women with all the strength they could summon. The wife was forced to do the cooking and kitchen work for the nine people in the house.

Turned Out

Then suddenly the boy husband fell ill of enteritis, due to the unsanitary conditions there, and was too weak to be removed. The girl-wife was left alone to fight the Beast 666. Since she defied him every way and managed to keep herself clear of the bestialities of the house, he turned her out one night. All that night she was unable to return into the "abbey" on the hills above Cefalù to tend her dying husband. Two days later the boy was dead.

The girl who had made so courageous a fight against the Beast who sought to destroy her was given money by the British Consul to return to England. Crowley was obliged to let her go. But he made dire threats of vengeance if she told what she knew.

She has not told anything more than has already been published in this newspaper, but she is still in danger from the Beast. The "Sunday Express" is putting the facts of this tragic case in the hands of Scotland Yard.

Child Spectators

It is among the clean minded and inexperienced that he seeks his victims. This latest tragedy has brought to light the fact that the Beast 666 has laid all plans for establishing a colony of Oxford youths at Cefalù, knows how to word them enticingly, and leaves out any hint of the unspeakable facts of his "religion" until such time as he has his victims fairly in his clutches.

The facts are too unutterably filthy to be detailed in a newspaper, for they have to do with sexual orgies that touch the lowest depth of depravity. The whole is mixed up in a hocus-pocus of doubtful mysticism, of which Crowley is "the Purple Priest."

Children under ten, whom the Beast keeps at the "abbey," are made to witness horrible sexual debauches unbelievably revolting. Filthy incense is burned and cakes made of goats' blood and honey are consumed in the windowless room where the Beast conducts his rites. The rest of the time he lies in a room hung with obscene pictures collected all over the world, saturating himself with drugs.

The Beast's Hope

An interesting piece of information has just reached the "Sunday Express." Crowley has outgrown the "abbey" at Cefalù. He desires to extend his activities, but lacks the money to do so. He put the problem before some of the spirits that attend his magic rites.

"Sue the 'Sunday Express' for £5,000 and build a new 'abbey' with the money" came the command.

The Beast foresaw difficulties. He could not risk bringing suit himself, for all the statements made in the newspaper were correct. If they had not been he would have brought suit long ago. Yet the "spirit" was insistent.

"£5,000 for a new abbey!"

So the Beast is sending one of his women to London to see what she can do.

The "Sunday Express" promises Crowley that it intends to pursue its investigations with the utmost ruthlessness, and that next Sunday it will endeavour to supply him with considerable further material on which to base any action which he may care to bring.

The worst paragraph in this "ruthless" journalistic orgy, in my opinion, is the final sneer against Crowley's inability to take legal action. Analysed, of course, the sneer is no more than a boast of the newspaper's wealth. The *Sunday Express* knew very well that Crowley was materially defenceless, at that time, against slanderous attacks in London, however false; for he had actually written to Lord Beaverbrook in those terms immediately after the DRUG FIEND "revelations." In the same letter Crowley had asked his Lordship for an independent inquiry into the charges, in the interests of fair play. This letter was never acknowledged. I take my facts from a little brochure by one of Crowley's friends, Norman Mudd, M.A., which was circulated at the time.

There is no need to clog the pages with much more of the filthy abuse of Crowley, the journalistic "sensational orgy" which followed Raoul Lovedays's death. It can easily be imagined from what has already been quoted; or the reader may consult the files of the *Sunday Express* if he enjoys orgiastic journalism. I quote here merely the opening paragraphs of the second of the interviews with Betty May in order to show the tone of the whole:

Sunday Express.   *March 4, 1923.*
YOUNG WIFE'S STORY
OF CROWLEY'S ABBEY.
SCENES OF HORROR.
DRUGS, MAGIC, AND VILE PRACTICES.
Girl's Ordeal.
Saved by the Consul.
With a full sense of the responsibility involved, the "Sunday Express" to-day publishes the story of the

young wife who has just returned from the "abbey" of Aleister Crowley in Sicily.

Last Sunday we told of the death of the girl's husband, a brilliant scholarship 'varsity graduate. For the sake of the lad's parents his name is withheld, and is today.

Sinister Figure

This man Crowley is one of the most sinister figures of modern times. He is a drug fiend, an author of vile books, the spreader of obscene practices. Yet such is his intellectual attainment and mental fascination that he is able to secure reputable publishers for his works and attract to him men and women of means and position.

The young wife is known to the artistic world as "Betty." She married her husband when he came down from Oxford.

Shortly after they met Crowley. Her husband, like many other undergraduates was interested in magic. Crowley fascinated him. He offered the young man a position as private secretary at his "abbey." The wife fought against it, but finally accompanied her husband there.

There were several more columns of nonsensical "interview" with Betty May, whose vivid imagination, conjoined with that of the reporters, touched up, one presumes, by the editorial department, made a pretty piece of balderdash.

Only *John Bull*, silliest of English journals, continued to exploit the canards in England. Readers would not thank me for reprinting any of the *John Bull* articles in full. A few headlines and a few purple patches from the numerous *John Bull* articles will suffice:

THE KING OF DEPRAVITY	*(March 10, 1923)*
THE WICKEDEST MAN IN THE WORLD	*(March 24, 1923)*
KING OF DEPRAVITY ARRIVES	*(April 14, 1923)*
WE TRAP THE TEMPTRESS	*(April 28, 1923)*
A CANNIBAL AT LARGE	*(April, 1923)*
A MAN WE'D LIKE TO HANG	*(May, 1923)*
A HUMAN BEAST RETURNS	*(August 30, 1924)*

Two of this series of articles shatteringly asserted that Crowley was actually in London, and clamoured for his immediate arrest, though Crowley was still abroad, all the time.

John Bull was obviously merely embroidering the "exposures" of the *Sunday Express*. A specimen purple patch is as follows:

> There are, however, other "activities" at the Abbey which admit of more detailed accusation. One of these is the method employed by Crowley of paying his numerous debts on the island, by sending out his women as "hostages" to those who are willing to accept this despicable method of payment.
>
> Another, which has considerably our inquiries and is even calculated to baffle the inquiries which have already been instituted by the Home Office and by Scotland Yard, is Crowley's practice of getting certain prominent and highly placed citizens of Cefalù and Palermo up to his "Abbey," where they are persuaded to take part in the sexual orgies which follow drug parties, and which even form a leading part in the Abbey's religious ceremonies."

We shall not hesitate to hand to the authorities the name of some of these distinguished visitors, together with further sworn testimony if, as we anticipate, a certain official on the Island endeavors to stifle Government investigations.

Suffice to say for the moment, that one of Crowley's women in the "Abbey" is shortly expecting another child to be born, the father of which is known to be a prominent banker in Palermo, who is a friend of the British Consul.

We may mention that, up to the time of this article going to press, no death certificate has been received by the relatives of the young Oxford graduate who died under such mysterious circumstances at the Abbey four weeks ago, nor has any reply been received from the British Consul at Palermo to the anxious inquiries made the young man's mother and sister concerning the death.

(March 24, 1923.)

The "cannibal" incident is as follows:

"Possessed at one time of ample private means, he penetrated into the recesses of Egypt, Algiers, Morocco, India, Burma, Siam, Mexico, Japan, and China, the East Indies, even into the "Forbidden Country" of Thibet. Concerning these travels and his various hunting expeditions some amazing stories are told, which Crowley himself is never tired of relating.

One of these is that leaving his camp in Kashmire one morning, unattended even by natives, Crowley returned with the statement that he had that morning killed two tigers, *single-handed*, one of which, by way of evidence, he carried—or dragged—back with him to camp! The natives of these parts of India visited by Crowley assert that he really had the power of cowing and killing wild beasts by some magical means.

On one solitary mountain-climbing expedition it is actually affirmed that running short of provisions, he killed two of his native carriers, and cut them up for food! This incredible piece of cannibalism is cynically authenticated by "The Beast" himself....

(April, 1923)

This kind of thing is bad enough, but the following piece of simplicity would take some beating:

Gradually things began to leak out at Cefalù, and one of the consequences was, after our articles had reached Italy, a raid by the local police. The Abbey was searched for opium and other drugs, but the search was unsuccessful.

Crowley was rather pleased. He was able to point out to his followers how easily he had duped the police, and the seances were renewed with every circumstance of blasphemous indecency.

(May 19, 1923.)

The journalistic methods of *John Bull* are of course sufficiently well known to be negligible in their effect precisely because of such crudity of statement as is exemplified in the foregoing extracts. It is perhaps the best possible commentary upon the journalistic good taste of James Douglas and *á fortiori*

Lord Beaverbrook, that only *John Bull* saw anything worthy of emulation in their slanders against the poet. However, foreign papers cannot be expected to make the appreciation of English journalistic values which English readers habitually make. All over the world the slanders against Crowley were reprinted sensationally. A few specimen headlines from American papers are here reproduced, taken in each case from full-page articles, fantastically and elaborately illustrated:

DRIVEN TO SUICIDE BY DEVIL WORSHIPPERS
Wicked Exploits of "The Ace of Spades," a Secret Organization Which Preys Upon Superstitious Women and Blackmails Them or Frightens Them to Death by Making Them Believe That Satan Owns Them.

SECRETS BEHIND THE SCENES
AMONG THE DEVIL-WORSHIPPERS
A Young English Bride Who Fled from the Sicilian "Abbey" of the Vicious New "Do Whatever You Want" Religion, Reveals the Wicked Rituals Carried On by Its "High Priest" and His Worshippers.

THE ANGEL CHILD WHO
"SAW HELL" AND CAME BACK.
Heartfelt Confessions of the London Art Model Who Turned Apache and Took to Drugs, and How a Genuine Vision Redeemed Her at the Brink.

What is perhaps more serious is that the "story" was also widely circulated in Continental papers, including the Italian Press. Probably as a result, Mussolini, who was at that time waging war against "Secret Societies," decided to expel Crowley from Italian territory. A petition was drawn up and signed by all the leading inhabitants of Cefalù, who were under no misapprehension with regard to Crowley, who was indeed one of them and was universally esteemed. Nevertheless, he had to go; a fact which caused the *Sunday Express* to gloat triumphantly, as might be expected. He went to Tunis and continued to write his *magnum opus*—his Autobiography of 600,000 words—under a previously made contract with his London publishers. After what had happened, however, the publishers were unwilling to proceed. Crowley therefore went to Paris and arranged for the printing of an imposing technical work on "Magick," which he had been engaged in writing for many years. While seeing this through the press, he was suddenly visited by the French police, who regarded with the utmost suspicion a coffee machine in his possession, believing it to be either and instrument for distilling drugs, or an anarchist bomb. Though nothing more incriminating was found against him, except for the technical "crime" that his identity card was out of date, Crowley was refused permission to remain in France; and he is now in England.

Here the story ends, so far as I am concerned. I have tried throughout to state the facts dispassionately. There can scarcely be any denying that the calumny of Crowley has gone too far. How much Crowley is himself responsible, I must leave it to the reader to judge; and the positive indignity of allowing a scurrilous attack to made upon a private individual deprived of the opportunity to rebut allegations in the same medium and with the same amount of space. The case against Lord Beaverbrook and James Douglas was clearly stated in Mr. Norman Mudd's pamphet. This pamphlet had a small private circulation, and has done something to rehabilitate Crowley in the eyes of a few people who thought "there must be something in it all" at a time of the worst "exposures." If the present work continues that process of rehabilitation, it will not have been in vain. A very few people will envy me the job I set myself of "whitewashing" Aleister Crowley's record. I do not look forward with any pleasure myself to the possibility of being tarred with the same brush because of the thankless task I have undertaken. At the same time, there is a possibility at least after the publication of this book, that intelligent people will form a truer estimate of the case concerning an English man of letters whose literary achievement is undeniable, whatever else may be said or rumoured.

Epilogue

Everything is constantly changing yet all remains exactly the same. The Stephensen text of this book together with my Introduction written in 1969 indicate that book reviewers and only reviewers and their point of view, rarely change. When Messrs. Hill & Wang of New York published *The Confessions of Aleister Crowley* in 1970, they asked me if I would care to appear on some of the television talk shows to advertise the book. I am ashamed to admit that I declined. Aleister Crowley is not an easy person to discuss in a conventional society over the air, especially if the interviewer is loaded down with his own prejudices taken over from the past. Any protagonist would look like an idiot and at that time I did not want to take a chance on that.

Nevertheless, at my request Hill & Wang sent me duplicates of every American book review they could lay hands on. For that, I am deeply obliged. My intention had been to incorporate these modern reviews in this postscript, if the sales of *The Legend Of Aleister Crowley* had been ample enough to warrant a second edition. Unfortunately, like the first edition of the early thirties, it merely languished on the vine. It remains to be seen now whether, with the eighties upon up, (The eighties cower and are abased before me.) a new era of at least some respect for the monumental work of Crowley is about to dawn. I am not really sure at this moment. For although more of his previously unpublished writing has appeared in one form or another, and though the modern social situation is far different from that of forty years ago, much of the old unthinking prejudice about him still persists like a heavy miasma in stagnant air.

Neither John Symonds or Kenneth Grant, the present editors of the *Confessions*, have done much to alleviate this. Symonds' malicious biography entitled *The Beast*, and Grant's egotism about being the head of the O.T.O. (which he is not and never has been) have only made matters worse. Neither do very much to lift up the consciousness of the so-called writers who do book reviews.

Still, there are a couple of notices in the mass of the 1970 material which Hill & Wang forwarded me which are worthy of attention. At the time of issuance, they may not have raised much of a storm, but a second look may be of interest to the youngster of today who has not had the chance of reading the original material or undergone the process of being poisoned psychologically by the emotional plague which some of the older reviewers spewed forth.

One of the most pleasant surprises I have just had, after going through this mass of material (which has been hidden for some ten or more years) was to find a review written by

Alan Watts of Zen fame in the San Francisco Examiner dated February 28, 1970. He has written a mass of diverse and well-penned literature on the Eastern Wisdom Religions, earning him an enviable reputation. In that review he speaks of Crowley, Rasputin, and Gurdjieff, et al. "I will call them inspired and genuine charlatans or *rascal masters*—people who were gurus of remarkable power and spirituality and yet, by Christian standards, were immoral or grossly ill-mannered...Crowley had the nerve to write this *autohagiography* or a biography of a saint—a volume which from beginning to end is almost entirely fascinating, witty, arrogant, immodest, and yet curiously wise...

"...the final, occult, unmentionable and esoteric secret of the *rascal masters* is simple: Follow nature and do just what you feel like doing—without hesitation, guilt or regret.... Crowley's autobiography is just one man's experiment in finding what he wanted...and the story is bizarre to an extreme... Yet some few considered him a Buddha.

"For myself, I make no judgment." So said Alan Watts. "It is possible that a man can be such a fraud as to be an incomparable and magical fraud. It is also possible that a man of high compassion and wisdom can play at being a fraud so as not to become an idol or the founder of a formal religion. Great and powerful men, in the religious dimension, are invariably regarded gods by some and as devils by others."

From one who is a research Fellow at the Bollingen Foundation, and the esteemed author of perhaps a dozen of first rate scholarly books, this is the highest insight possible. It does more to damn the conventional, prosaic and all too common type of bourgeois reviews appearing during the past fifty years to impress a more informed public that here is a man—not merely *the wickedest man in the world* but a spiritual genius who knew what he was about no less than the most illuminated and hard headed Zen Roshi.

In much the same way, and in the same collection of what can only be termed junk reviews that Hill & Wang sent me a dozen years ago, there is another unforgettable piece of good writing. Robert Anton Wilson is a *mindblower* of the finest kind. Some years ago, he wrote a slim volume called *The Cosmic Trigger*. It *blew my mind* so completely that I must have bought nearly three dozen copies to give to some of my dearest friends and former patients. Most of them replied enthusiastically, stating that reading it had so excited them as to keep many of them awake for several nights. It was one of the most stimulating experiences many had had in years.

In *The Realist*, dated September-October 1971, the editors must have given Wilson carte blanche to review *The Confessions* as it should be reviewed, in some nine or ten full length magazine pages. I was almost moved to request permission to quote the entire thing—every line, every word. But that clearly was impossible. But apart from the review by Watts, it is the only one that even begins to exhibit any appreciation of the intellectual and spiritual subtlety of Crowley in any capacity—as a writer of superb English, a great mystic, a fine poet (contrary to most current opinion) a mountaineer of daring and extraordinary skill.

"Friends and disciples celebrated his funeral with a Black Mass, or so the newspapers said" wrote Wilson flippantly. "Actually, it was a Gnostic Catholic Mass (even John Symonds, Crowley's most hostile biographer, admits that at most it could be called a Grey Mass, not a Black Mass—observe the racist and Christian chauvinist implications in this terminology) but it was certainly not an orthodox R.C. or Anglican mass. I mean, cripes, the priestess took off her clothes in one part of it, buck naked, and they call that a Mass, glorioski!"

As an aside Bobby Mather in the Detroit Free Press said: "Today, Crowley with his mind-expanding drugs, his incense, bells, robes and incantations, his I Ching Hexagrams and his studies of Eastern and Western Mysticism, would be just another one of the boys in any hippie pad. The group sex, practiced by his disciples at his temple in Sicily, which finally led to his expulsion from Italy, might rate a paragraph in some newspapers in 1970."

Connolly Cole in Panorama - Chicago Daily News, dated March 14-15, 1970, wrote "Variously a mountain climber, poet, writer, explorer, world-traveler and an inveterate disciple of arcana, Crowley presents himself in this extravaganza as the veritable reincarnation of the all-round Renaissance man, reflected in an extraordinary literary style that is pure conceit. His life was largely shallow and selfish. Yet his athletic claims appear justified—he was in fact a mountaineer of more than ordinary skill—amid the incessant burps of ego that propelled him through life until his frail death at the age of 75 in a faded boarding house in a less than fashionable part of England... Despite his noisy escapades, he remained the product of his upbringing. He had a felicitous sense of wickedness without the ability to achieve it...He was avid for symbols and sacrificial rites, although the occasional immolation of a passing goat seemed to satiate such infatuations that were, in their innocence, redolent more of innocuous parlor games than of perilous occult pursuits." Now we can return to Robert Anton Wilson. The preceding bits of review only tend to highlight what he and Alan Watts had to say about a man of whom they had taken full measure, whereas the others saw only a nonentity of their own kind. Wilson goes on at great length discussing almost every phase of Crowley's philosophy, magick, the problem of good and evil, and everything else that Crowley had written about. But he ends his treatise (not the review) with a very long paragraph as follows:

"And yet—and yet—Manson reminds us, our brothers and sisters in the Movement remind us, sometimes our own unexpected behaviour reminds us: there have been such millennial voices in the past and they have been heralds not of a Golden Dawn but only a false dawn.

"If there is one central lesson to be learned from the Beast, it is not really Do what thou will shall be the whole of Law (which has been around since Rabelais), not even the more profound and gnomic Every man and every woman is a Star:

not even the formula of the Perfect Orgasm for which Norman Brown has been searching so loudly and forlornly lo! these many years; it is rather his humor, his skepticism, his irony that revelled in the title of Beast and, even, at times, Ass; the rationality that warned against becoming *the prey of madness* by trusting one's visions too quickly, and the common sense which said that, even if good and evil are identical on the Absolute plane, a man operating on the relative plane simply doesn't enjoy a toothache or invent rationalizations to pick a brother's pocket; the solemn warning that the sacrament is not completed until the Magician offers *the last drop of his life's blood* to the Cup, and dies; but, above all of these, the simple historical record which reveals that with all the ardor, all the dedication, all the passion he possessed, it still took eight years (including four month's madness) before he threw down the wall that separates Ego from true Self and that Self from the Universe.

Wilson's humor is at his best also in this long treatise on Crowley—but his humor, though apparently leveled at Crowley, is in reality directed at the general public which damned him. This can be furthered demonstrated by his introduction to my *Eye In The Triangle*, Falcon Press, 1982. "Listen, some critic (I forgot who) wrote of Lugosi 'acting with total sincerity and a kind of demented cornball poetry' and the words, like the old crimson-lined black cape, seemed tailored equally well for the shoulders of the Master Therion, To Mega Therion, the Great Beast, Aleister Crowley. This is the final degradation 'this avatar of anarchy, this epitome of rebellion, this incarnation of inconsistency, this man Crowley whom his contemporaries called *The King of Depravity, The Wickedest Man in the World, A Cannibal at Large, A Man We'd Like to Hang, A Human Beast* and with some anti-climax, *A Pro-German and Revolutionary*.

"Now, to us, he is quaint. Worse: he is Camp. Worse yet, he is corny. We don't even believe his boast that he performed human sacrifice 150 times a year starting in 1912.

"None of these cordial titles were invented by myself. All were used, in Crowley's life-time, by the newspaper *John Bull*, in its heroic and nigh-interminable campaign to save England from the Beast's pernicious influence." So much for Wilson.

The New York Times of January 17, 1970, had a review by Thomas Lask with the subtitle of *Vanity, Vision and a Few Vices*. On the whole however, Lask was not altogether unappreciative of Crowley as were the great majority of the other common-place American reviewers, far too numerous to notice here. He starts off the review with "It would be too easy to give the back of the hand to this long, long-winded and sometimes incoherent exercise in personal panegyric. The unending stream of self-praise begins to sound like a caricature of itself. The continual assertion of success in occult matters brings on its own skepticism. The lofty soul-like language used to describe each new sexual encounter becomes as transparent as a Hollywood blurb. The assertive assurance of a young man slowly changes to the whiny bleating of an old one. The dark mysteries that he describes, invents and explicates are opaque film that obscures large chunks of this autobiography...

"In a small way, the Crowley of the *Confessions* asserts himself against our own age. In a time of angst, of alienation, of dislocated generations, when so many of use are afraid that the centre will not hold. Crowley has a calm certainty of his own worth, an assurance of his own genius, a confidence in his own actions that raise a schoolboy's cheer in the mind of the reader. He exhibits an arrogance and a snobbishness that carry things off by their own daring. He may suffer from an excess of these qualities, but he has all the markings of an underground hero."

So Lask does not damn him entirely as do so many others. On the other hand, he winds up the review with "If nothing has been said here about Crowley's voluminous writings and comments on magic, various occult orders, freemasonry, ultra-phenomenal experiences and the like, it is only that they are a bog in which the uninitiate is sure to sink and disappear. The *Confessions* which could use some rigorous editing, is not an unalloyed pleasure, and some will find the book intolerable. But the metamorphoses of the human personality that it reveals will always remain to intrigue and tease us."

The very staid Library Journal of February 15, 1970 surprised me a little bit by being as objective as such a journal could possibly hope to be. So there is always hope.

"Crowley...always a strong-minded man, sex-driven and hedonistic, developed an intensely hypnotic personality. He was creatively literate, a chess master, and an expert mountaineer and explorer adventurer in many lands. His dominating personality attracted a limited but world wide following, while his well-known debaucheries infuriated contemporaries, and governments alike—there are similarities to our hippie generation...

"This *Book of the Law*...satisfies many of his followers and may, indeed, interest other people today, for he wrote—as many of our own youth sincerely proclaim—'As a God goes, I go.' And, as the editors comment, he used the I Ching for probing the future long before that work became popular in intellectual circles in the West. Thus because of the relevance of Crowley's philosophies to the present scene, this may readily become one of the most widely read autobiographies of the next few years."

One of the loveliest of the really long and penetrating reviews that did appear around this time was written by Nigel Dennis entitled *Marks of a Buddha* which appeared in the New York Review on March 12, 1970. It is a fine, penetrating approach interspersed here and there with humor and sarcasm, but never with rancor or with the ignorance so characteristic of the great majority I have in my hand.

Dennis opens up with "I find no fault in this man, said Pontius Pilate on a certain occasion, and I must follow him on the present occasion. I find no fault at all in the book under review: if it was not sent into this world to redeem man it was sent certainly to fill man with hilarity..." After quoting Crowley's description of Gerald Kelly, his brother in law, the reviewer notes that it reminds him that "Crowley did confess to one fatal flaw in his own character 'a fatal weakness for believing the best about everybody.' I don't believe this consisted in his being too English. I have no basic objection to a man being English; it gives him a confidence that one looks for in vain among people of other nations, he remarks "And in what book but an English book could one read such a line as 'I...went to stay with Allan, who had been advanced from a simple bikkhu to a sayadaw in his choung...?

"No, the trouble only starts when this English naturalness is smirched by foreign influences. One cannot, as Crowley did, make *Rule Britannia!* a favorite song and hope at the same time to attain to 'Sammasati, Right Recollection, the seventh step on the Noble Eightfold Path...'

"Personally, I prefer his men friends to his women; they are more interesting. There is a man from Bridgeport, Conn., who has the paltry *Americanized* signature Samuel A. Jacob, but soon proves to be no other than SHMUEL Bar AIWAZ bin YACKOU de SHERABAD. There is something in this connection also about the O.T.O's magical formula which in some manner incarnated the Lost World of Freemasonry with the value of 418, 'the number of the Magical Formula of the Aeon.' I like the Grand Treasurer of the Ordo Templi Orientis, who was a deaf mute...he and the Grand Secretary hopped off with all the Order's money while Crowley was initiating a certain Sister Cypris into passions 'no less fierce than anything in Wuthering Heights'...Best of all the men, however is Eckenstein, the German-born mountaineer from Oxford, with whom

Crowley attempted to climb Kanchenjunga and made a very thorough exploration of the mountains of Mexico. Eckenstein was to Crowley what Wittgenstein has been to Oxford, and it is sad to read that after recurrent attacks of 'spasmodic asthma' he was carried off in his prime by the deadly combination of 'phthisis and marriage.' I would give a lot for a book called *Crowley's Gesprache mit Eckenstein*.

"Crowley was an Englishman of the old school, and I believe that if he had not been corrupted by Uncle Tom he would have made a first class administrator of natives. He liked robes and processions; he loved mountains and wild places; he took promptly to bizarre religions; he knew that if Indians were allowed to attend the London School of Economics they would go to bed with English girls and bust the Empire from the bottom up. The danger is that the way of life he chose may be imitated by **little men** who have none of his character and originality and who suppose that with little effort they may become, as he became, first a Magus, then a Saint, and finally God.... The strong prose, the hilarious stories, the superb self-confidence—these are just as apparent after Crowley became God as they were when he was only a Saint. Criticism, in my opinion, is never just when it shows signs of envy."

A trivia entitled the *Egoist* in the Courier-Post of Camden, N.J., March 11, 1970 is simply idiotic after the above. The reviewer, Frank Funk wrote "What a shock it must be to a man who during the course of his life thwarted demons, wrestled with the devil, conversed with those as familiar with the cabbala as any sixth grader with the multiplication tables, to be unable to thwart the angel of death." (This may indicate that Frank Funk is himself in a blue funk about dying!)

Another kind of contemptuous approach was essayed by Julian Mitchel in the New York Times Book Review on February 22, 1970. It begins interestingly enough, but gradually winds down to pure tripe. The second paragraph sounds as if it might amount to something, but it peters out quickly. "When high-minded clergymen can defend D. H. Lawrence in the English courts on the grounds that sex may be a Christian sacrament, no one is likely to dare to protest against the description of drug trips (or stumbles) as 'valid' mystical experiences. We don't know where in heaven or hell we are. We live in the age of Aleister Crowley, the Beast 666, magus, mountaineer and bore...

"He wrote incessantly and badly, publishing his books at his own expense, and worked his way sure-footed up the ladder of the Hermetic Order of the Golden Dawn. He saw visions and took drugs and experimented wildly; it's very hard to tell how much he believed in what he was doing. A friend became a Buddhist monk, but Crowley was not amenable to discipline..."

This shows how little he knew of the history of this man who spent the greater part of his life mastering the disciplines of a host of mystic systems.

"The editors are very sparing in their comments on the claims made in the book, but I think we can be sure that nothing whatever can be taken on trust. Somewhere, the *Confessions* are presumably going to be essential reading; our chaos is such that no folly is too great to be sanctified by someone...But the most astonishing thing about the book is that it is being published at all. Crowley died in 1947. His reputation was already faded then. Who cares about him now, in England or America? Reluctantly, I have to admit that probably lots of people do.

"Aleister Crowley wasn't superman; he was an absurd bore of a particular English kind, the man who lives for being a 'gentleman'—which no real gentleman, naturally, ever does. He is the apotheosis of the amateur. His prose is all pomp and circumstance, just as his verse is all Swinburne. His vehement boasting rings in the ears like a beggar's whine. He is a snob, and like all snobs, suffers from terrible social insecurity...This vast tome should settle his reputation once and for all. It is a sharp stake through the heart of the Beast 666. But God knows what monsters are stalking in his steps." The New York Times sure knows how to pick book reviewers!

The Detroit Free Press is not much better, though Bobby Mather, their reviewer, is a bit more amusing than a hundred others. "One can view Crowley in many ways; as a seeker after ultimate truth, or as a deluded degenerate, or as a man in the grip of powerful unconscious forces, or as a posturing fool. But 'Do what thou wilt' was the whole of his law, and at least he practiced what he preached. Whether he was the last of the Red-Hot Magicians, or the first of the Red-Hot Swingers, he was, nevertheless, fascinating."

Melvin Maddocks in the Christian Science Monitor of around the same time is not very much better than Bobby Mather. He wrote: "Life started out more or less straight for young Aleister. He was a Cambridge man and a proper aesthete. Silk shirts, floppy ties, and so on. And he scribbled the obligatory slim book of verse. But then Aleister went odd... Crowley comes closer to being a buffoon-rebel, a stock company version of Milton's Lucifer with the courage to state his own pathos: 'I did not see why I should be confined to one life.' At least once in this life, he spoke for Everyman.

The reviewer in LIFE was at least really funny. "The many fascinating pictures which adorn The Confessions of St. Crowley show a man who looks like a cross between a French convict, a solid English country gentleman and someone playing Pooh-Bah in the varsity Mikado. Was this the face that scaled the Himalayas and sent women careening into alcoholism and suicide? Was this the face that pops up as one of the 'people we like' on the Beatles' Sgt. Pepper album!

"Back to Voltaire, kids, before it's too late."

This was written by Richard Freedman, an author and critic who teaches English at Simmons College. I hope we hear from him again!

Thus ends this postscript to the *Legend of Aleister Crowley*. There is every indication that the old Legend is still very much alive, with only the vaguest hint that intelligent comment and criticism have made a dent in the asinine views of the reviewers — and so of the general public.

The reviews in this Legend go back almost eighty years. We still find the same set of slurs, repudiations, and insults that were prevalent then. That Crowley endured them, even though the development of some bitterness was covered up by his magnificent humor, is a tribute to his fortitude, his spiritual experience, and some sense of Mission.

My hope still remains that the Legend of Aleister Crowley and the books that Crowley wrote will not remain merely for a discerning few, but that their effects will ripple outwards again and again to fertilize an age that quite evidently is about to undergo eclipse. As his Book of the Law said, and which he himself never quite understood, 'I am the warrior Lord of the Forties: the Eighties cower before me & are abased.'

We shall see!

Israel Regardie
Arizona

New Falcon Publications
**Publisher of Controversial Books and CDs
Invites You to Visit Our Website:
http://www.newfalcon.com**

At the Falcon website you can:

- Browse the online catalog of all our great titles, including books by Robert Anton Wilson, Christopher S. Hyatt, Israel Regardie, Aleister Crowley, Timothy Leary, Osho, Lon Milo DuQuette, and many more
- Find out what's available and what's out of stock
- Get special discounts
- Order our titles through our secure online server
- Find products not available anywhere else including:
    - One of a kind and limited availability products
    - Special packages
    - Special pricing
- And much, much more

PN 2080 .N45 2005
WITHDRAWN
New audition scenes and
monologs from contemporary

JAN 2007

DATE DUE

APR 2 4 2007	
MAR 2 7 2007	
APR 1 0 2008	
MAR 1 3 2008	
DEC 0 1 2008	
JAN 1 4 2009	
MAR 2 0 2009	
OCT 2 6 2010	
OCT 0 7 2010	OCT 0 7 2010
JAN 0 4 2012	
DEC 0 7 2011	
GAYLORD	PRINTED IN U.S.A.

Parkland College Library
2400 West Bradley Avenue
Champaign, IL 61821